D0592089

Twayne's English Authors Series

Sylvia E. Bowman, *Editor*

INDIANA UNIVERSITY

John Gay

22

John Gay

By PATRICIA MEYER SPACKS

Wellesley College

Twayne Publishers, Inc. :: New York

Library of Congress Catalog Card Number: 65-18223

MANUFACTURED IN THE UNITED STATES OF AMERICA

For

Bertrand H. Bronson

Contents

Preface

As far as his literary reputation is concerned, it was John Gay's misfortune to have distinguished friends. The companion of Alexander Pope and Jonathan Swift, Gay has long been overshadowed by them, victim of the critical assumption that his literary aims were the same as theirs but his success far more limited.

To some extent, of course, this judgment is accurate enough. Yet the matter is not so simple: Gay's achievement requires the sort of detailed critical analysis that has long been denied him. Although two modern critics have provided thorough examinations of *The Beggar's Opera,* although a good deal of scholarly energy has been devoted to questions about Gay's sources, although James Sutherland has written a fine general essay on Gay, there remains only one book (Sven Armens, *John Gay, Social Critic*) which attempts to examine Gay's work as a whole. Even this study is limited to a consideration of the content of Gay's poetry with little reference to its form. Wallace Cable Brown, on the other hand, has studied in some detail Gay's use of the couplet, but the limitations of his point of view are partially suggested by his chapter title: "Gay: Pope's Alter Ego." There is, in short, a real need for a thorough critical survey of Gay's work. Such a survey this volume attempts to provide.

Gay's relative failures, as well as his successes as poet and playwright, are illuminating: through examining his experiments with subject, genre, and technique, one may often achieve clearer insight than that obtainable from Gay's surer contemporaries into some of the special challenges to creativity in eighteenth-century poetic practice. The scope of the books in this series forbids detailed analysis of the poet's relation to his time; yet Gay's work at every point reveals how the conventions governing eighteenth-century poetry provided for him both a problem and an important source of strength. It is Gay's persistent struggle to find an appropriate poetic stance—a proper emotional, intellectual, and moral perspective through which he might express himself powerfully in verse—that supplies the focus of the present study. The eighteenth-century assumption, for example, that direct expression of an author's feelings in poetry was not necessarily either significant or interesting has particular relevance to Gay's case; the value of the assumption is demonstrated by the poet's struggles with it, for Gay, speaking directly in his own voice, seems far less perceptive, far less the poet, than when he succeeds in producing utterances from behind a mask. Only by sacrificing directness was he able to achieve the complexity and richness of his best work.

The succeeding chapters will attempt to trace Gay's development chronologically through his literary production, treating poems and plays separately. This study should define the nature of the poet's progress: from hiding behind a mask to learning how to manipulate it successfully. The convention that an author must remove himself from his material in order to achieve the necessary authority for dealing with it was always troublesome to Gay; yet it is possible to discern in his work a gradually increasing, if only sporadically controlled, dexterity in using "distance" to fruitful purpose. In such early poems as *Rural Sports,* one perceives the embarrassed young man alternately trying to dodge responsibility for his predilections toward country life and attempting to justify them. Later, in *Trivia,* Gay came to see more clearly the necessity for complicated perspective, through which he was able to provide often striking insights into the meaning and value of life in the city. Finally, with a technique more complicated still, the poet returned to naïveté, used now as his most successful disguise. As the writer of animal fables, as the poet-beggar in *The Beggar's Opera,* Gay was able to deal in simplicities with great sophistication: the mask of the naïf was far more valuable to him than actual naïveté.

This study will be concerned to examine both Gay's perceptions and the forms in which he embodied them, for Gay's work is interesting in itself, not merely in relation to its time or in contrast to the work of his greater contemporaries. The poet has much to say to the twentieth century; the charm and ease with which, at his best, he communicates makes it a pleasure to linger over his verse. He appears not to take himself seriously; he seems to invite us not to take him seriously; then suddenly he turns out to be, after all, disingenuous, to reveal the flash of perception which sheds new light.

My great debt to the teacher who first revealed to me the excitement and complexity of eighteenth-century poetry is acknowledged by my dedication. More specifically, I am indebted to George Slover, who made valuable suggestions about my treatment of Gay's plays, and to my husband, who proved himself once more a patient, perceptive and indefatigable editor.

Chronology

1685 June 30, John Gay born in Barnstaple.
1695? Gay attends Barnstaple Grammar School, where he is friendly with William Fortescue and Aaron Hill.
1702? Goes to London as apprentice to silk mercer.
1706 Quits apprenticeship, returns briefly to Barnstaple.
1707? Goes back to London, becomes secretary to Aaron Hill.
1708 *Wine* is published.
1711 *The Present State of Wit* published. By this time Gay has met Pope.
1712 *The Mohocks* published. Gay becomes domestic steward in household of the Duchess of Monmouth.
1713 *Rural Sports* published. *The Wife of Bath* produced. *The Fan* published. Four poems included in Steele's *Poetical Miscellanies.* Gay becomes secretary of Scriblerus Club.
1714 *The Shepherd's Week* published. Gay goes on diplomatic mission to Hanover as secretary to Lord Clarendon; Queen Anne's death ends appointment. *A Letter to a Lady* published.
1715 Gay visits Exeter at Lord Burlington's expense. Writes "Epistle to Burlington." *The What d'ye Call It* produced and published.
1716 *Trivia* published; "The Toilette" included in *Court Poems.*
1717 *Three Hours After Marriage* produced and published. Gay visits Paris and Aix with the Pulteneys.
1719 Gay is again on the Continent.
1720 *Poems on Several Occasions* (including *Dione*) published; Gay makes a large profit from volumes, but loses much of it in the South Sea Bubble.
1721 *A Panegyrical Epistle to Mr. Thomas Snow* published. Gay spends a good deal of time with Lord Burlington and with the Duchess of Queensberry.

1723 Gay is made Commissioner of State Lottery. Reads *The Captives* to the Princess of Wales.
1724 *The Captives* produced and published. Gay spends time in Lord Burlington's household, then has holiday at Bath with Dr. Arbuthnot.
1725 *To a Lady on her Passion for Old China; Newgate's Garland* published. Gay attempts to win court preferment. Begins work on *Fables.*
1727 *Fables* published. Gay is offered appointment as gentleman-usher to Princess Louise, but declines.
1728 *The Beggar's Opera* produced and published; enormously successful. Gay makes large profit. Writes *Polly,* which is not allowed to be acted.
1729 *Polly* published. Duchess of Queensberry banished from court for soliciting subscriptions there; Duke also leaves court. Gay loses apartments in Whitehall, lives with Queensberrys. *Polly* is widely pirated, but brings in large income.
1730 *The Wife of Bath* produced and published.
1732 *Acis and Galatea* produced, with music by Handel. Libretto alone published. December 3, Gay dies. Buried in Westminster Abbey, December 23.
1733 *Achilles* produced and published.
1734 *The Distress'd Wife* produced.
1738 *Fables,* Vol. II, published.
1743 *The Distress'd Wife* published.
1754 *The Rehearsal at Goatham.*
1777 *Polly* first produced.
1820 *Gay's Chair* (poems purporting to be by Gay, but undoubtedly spurious).
1926 *The Beggar's Opera* revived in London, by Nigel Playfair, beginning the new wave of interest in Gay.
1963 New production of *The Beggar's Opera* in London.

John Gay

CHAPTER 1

Early Masks and Models

NOT until 1713, when he was twenty-eight years old, did John Gay begin to discover models which made extended poetic expression possible for him. He then described himself, in the first version of *Rural Sports*, as having "courted Bus'ness with successless Pain,/And in Attendance wasted Years in vain." For about eleven years he had struggled to make his way in London, having come from the provinces (Barnstaple, in Devon) as an apprentice to a silk mercer. When, around 1708, he became secretary to Aaron Hill, a minor playwright and magazine editor who briefly managed Drury Lane theater, he entered for the first time the literary world he yearned to be part of. Before 1713, however, he had published only one long poem, *Wine* (a work apparently too poor, in his opinion, to include in the collected poems seven years later), and a farcical play, *The Mohocks,* which he had been unable to get produced.

His vision of success, then as later, had to do with approval more than with accomplishment. For the patronage of the great he would dance attendance, never feeling that his rewards were adequate, yet always hopeful of winning some appointment, the symbol of success, or a gift, tangible sign of approval, or the warm glow of general admiration in which a poet might bask. His poetic resources were not impressive: a grammar school education, a first-hand knowledge of the country (which would not, in the early eighteenth century, provide a great deal of respectable poetic subject matter), a comparatively superficial and recent knowledge of the life of the town, and, of course, a strong desire to be a poet.

The path he should follow must have seemed rather clearly defined. A man who, in our own time, sets out to be a poet has above all the problem of originality: if he can readily be dismissed as an imitator, or as essentially indistinguishable in technique and subject from his contemporaries, he is unlikely to win recognition. He must, at the very least, follow Pound's dictum and "make it new." He must offer his own insights, make his voice seem a *special* one. In early eighteenth-century London the poetic situation was spectacularly different. Pope was soon to offer his famous definition in the *Essay on Criticism:*

> True wit is nature to advantage dressed:
> What oft was thought, but ne'er so well expressed.

The idea that a poet need say nothing new, need only say something true, well, was a commonplace of the age. Moreover, the "imitation" was itself a highly respected literary form: a young man could versify in English some Latin model, changing allusions for the sake of topicality, and the results would be recognized as fresh poetry.

Gay's first problem, then, was to choose appropriate models. Not only did he value classical sanctions for his utterances, he needed a point of view: to select a specific Latin model was to determine the poetic stance he would adopt, the perspective from which he would approach his material. And the problem of perspective was always to be crucial for John Gay, whose tolerance and amiability apparently made it difficult for him to assume the authority of a commentator on the human scene.

In 1713 the first version of *Rural Sports* was published and also *The Fan;* early the next year *The Shepherd's Week* appeared. These three poems, with the earlier *Wine,* comprise a sequence of increasingly elaborate attempts to employ respectable models; despite their obvious weaknesses, they also demonstrate some of Gay's important poetic resources. *Wine,* his first published work, soon forgotten even in its own time, nonetheless tells us a good deal about our poet. It was in conception actually third-hand: a parody of Milton which imitated two far more successful pieces in the same vein, John Philips' *Splendid Shilling* and *Cyder.* "The merit of such performances begins and ends with the first author," commented Dr. Johnson of *The Splendid Shilling.* "He that should again adapt Milton's phrase to the gross incidents of common life, and even adapt it with more art, which would not be difficult, must yet expect but a small part of the praise which Philips has obtained; he can only hope to be considered as the repeater of a jest."[1] *Wine,* which generally has been dismissed as only a repeated jest, can make few claims to real poetic merit, yet it demonstrates certain un-Miltonic characteristics which foretell a good deal about Gay's later poetry. The problems it manifests, although here more blatantly displayed, are those which were persistently to plague its author.

The piece is a burlesque account of the virtues of wine, considered as "the source/Whence human pleasures flow." In the first 186 lines Gay explains the emotional values of drinking, its importance to trade, its inspirational effect on poets, its association with the classical past; roughly the last hundred lines of the poem detail the progress of a modern evening of drinking.

When the burlesque mask drops, as it frequently does, the reader becomes suddenly conscious that Gay is not merely joking. He praises wine for checking "inglorious, lolling ease"—which, biographies and contemporary letters frequently assert, was his own besetting temptation; he describes how wine stimulates the circulation of the blood (11. 42-44); he even recounts, in emotively colored language, the end of the night of drinking and the stumbling trip homeward:

> Thus we the winged hours in harmless mirth
> And joys unsullied pass, till humid night
> Has half her race perform'd; now all abroad
> Is hush'd and silent, nor the rumbling noise
> Of coach or cart, or smoky link-boy's call
> Is heard—but universal Silence reigns:
> When we in merry plight, airy and gay,
> Surprised to find the hours so swiftly fly,
> With hasty knock, or twang of pendent cord,
> Alarm the drowsy youth from slumb'ring nod;
> Startled he flies, and stumbles o'er the stairs
> Erroneous, and with busy knuckles plies
> His yet clung eyelids, and with stagg'ring reel
> Enters confused, and mutt'ring asks our wills;
> When we with liberal hand the score discharge,
> And homeward each his course with steady step
> Unerring steers, of cares and coin bereft.
> (11. 256-72)

If the language and tone help to ridicule the "drowsy youth," for example, they do not entirely obscure the poet's real sympathy for him; the same language defines the precise nature of the drinkers' state, "of cares . . . bereft." Such sections reveal a use of elevated Miltonic diction for two contradictory purposes: to mock low concerns by treating them with high language, but also, at other moments, to dignify such matters by the language the poet applies to them. If he burlesques in the mode of Philips, he also praises in the mode of James Thomson, who in *The Seasons* was to elevate rural concerns partly by employing the language of Milton.

Miltonic diction here provided John Gay not with one perspective but with two; and the apparent lack of conviction in *Wine* comes partly from the resultant division of emphasis. The unmistakable note of sincerity dominates when Gay deals honestly with real reactions and feelings, speaking not of the artificial mythological associations of wine-drinking, but of its genuine effects—genuinely, if a trifle shamefacedly, perceived as valuable. *Wine* asserts—clumsily, deviously, yet vividly—the value of companionship, of talk, of vigor, of life itself. And the assertion that life was intrinsically interesting and valuable, although that assertion was often heavily disguised, was to become Gay's major poetic theme.

Equally significant in relation to Gay's later development is the extraordinary sense of vigor and movement which *Wine* frequently projects. Correlatives of this feeling of energy are not far to seek. Many of the ideas in the poem emerge through images of movement. *Wine* proceeds by a series of visions of rising, soaring, falling, sailing, clashing, fighting. Gay's muse is to soar with "no middle flight" (1. 13); the wine raises the "drooping fronts" of its drinkers (1. 42), who lift the glass so that the wine may glide "swiftly o're the Tongue" (1. 47). As a result, "The circling *Blood* with quicker motion flies" (1. 48). The repulsed lover, encouraged by wine, "*Storms* the Breach, and *Wins* the Beauteous Fort" (1. 67). The British seaman finds himself "plowing the Ocean" (1. 71), while his ship "Rides tilting ore the Waves" (1. 72). Wine stimulates the poet's muse until

aloft she towres
Born on stiff *Pennons,* and of Wars alarms,
And *Trophies* won, in loftiest Numbers sings.
(11. 106-08)

It enflames sluggish minds with generous fires (1. 112), engages the quickened soul (1. 113), causes yet another muse to soar aerial (11. 122-23), heightens wit (1. 144). Examples can be lavishly multiplied; the dominant tone of the poem is that of abounding energy.

This fact is surprising, when one considers the nature of Miltonic blank verse, particularly as perceived by its eighteenth-century imitators. In contrast to the heroic couplet, which was the poetic norm of the early 1700's, blank verse seemed a leisurely and comparatively undisciplined form. It did not demand the obvious control of the couplet; it did not encourage a verse of elaborate tensions and balances. When James Thomson, a few years after Gay, used Miltonic blank verse for serious purposes in *The Seasons,* Dr. Johnson was able to make a dramatic point by reading aloud only every other line. The effect, listeners agreed, was as coherent as blank verse could be expected to be. Moreover, Miltonic blank verse provided a particularly tempting model because its devices seemed to the unwary so obvious and so easy to imitate: the rolling Latinate words, the thunderous lists of exotic names, the convoluted grammatical constructions. All these techniques, obviously, would encourage a slow and ponderous pace, a tone the opposite of energetic.

And Gay uses them all, if only to parody them; they can be demonstrated within a few lines of *Wine*. The poet speaks, for example, of the sources of wine:

> Whether from *Formian* Grape depress'd, *Falern*
> Or *Setin, Massic, Gauran* or *Sabine,*
> *Lesbian* or *Caecuban*. . . .
>
> (11. 141-43)

The invocation of grape names mocks Milton's sonority and grandeur. Four lines later occurs a striking example of tortured construction and Latinate diction:

> But *we,* not as our Pristin sires, repair
> T'*umbrageous* Grot or Vale, but when the Sun
> Faintly from Western Skies his rays oblique
> Darts sloping, and to *Thetis* wat'ry Lap
> Hastens in Prone Career. . . .
>
> (11. 146-50)

Yet such passages, interesting for their expertise in parodying an old-fashioned mode, are so interspersed with moments or sequences of sheer enthusiasm that the total effect of *Wine* depends less on them than on a totally contradictory image of youthful life. The lines quoted above continue, "with Friends select/Swiftly we hie to Devil *Young* or *Old*. . . ." The Devil was a famous tavern of Gay's time; the jauntiness of the pun on "going to the devil" is thoroughly characteristic of Gay.

Wine, hardly a good enough poem to justify detailed critical examination, is a significant portent. Its confusions of attitude and emphasis, its alternations between vigor and mechanical imitation, reveal the poet's divided mind; its concern with feeling and its respect for simple pleasures suggest some of his central interests; its poetic skill and its ineptitudes indicate the difficulties of evaluating the work of John Gay.

II

Rural Sports demonstrates problems similar to those of *Wine,* but it is a far more interesting poem. In it Gay returned to the classics for a model to be used straightforwardly. Virgil's *Georgics* echo always behind the poem, which contains a lengthy tribute to its Virgilian source; moreover, as a modern critic has thoroughly demonstrated, Gay's drastic revision of *Rural Sports* in 1720 must have been at least partially intended to emphasize its georgic aspects.[2] In many ways Gay follows his master closely: in his stress on the theme of seasonal progression, in his emphasis on the contrast between city and country life, in his detailed instructions about how to pursue the activities he describes, in his concern with the welfare of animal life (to the very worm on the fish hook), even, as Aden points out (pp. 231-32), in the "magisterial tone" which he frequently adopts. But however closely it imitates a model, *Rural Sports* is peculiarly Gay's own—the more so, perhaps, for the sense of tradition it conveys. In it we can see clearly his early mastery of poetic techniques which later dominate poems of quite a different kind.

Rural Sports is dedicated to Pope—a young and rural Pope, not yet come to town from Windsor Forest. "You, who the sweets of rural life have known,/Despise th' ungrateful hurry of the town" (ll. 1-2). The dedication has, in the context of the poem as a whole, profound appropriateness. It is used most immediately, however, as a preamble to some lines of conventionalized self-pity: Gay envies Pope his capacity merely to enjoy himself and the muse in his rural retreat, and he contrasts Pope's lot with his own, as "Long in the noisie town . . . . immur'd" (l. 11).

The organization of the poem is simple. After the opening passage, Gay indicates certain general advantages of country living, including the fact that the country provides an appropriate environment in which to read the *Georgics*. He suggests the progress of the day and then that of the seasons, moving thus into his central subject: the sports appropriate to various seasons. Spring is sacred to fishing, whose techniques and excitements the poet thoroughly displays. Autumn calls him to hunting, depicted in almost equal detail. And the poem concludes with a lengthy panegyric on the joys of country living, in which the "happy fields" are finally "The kind rewarders of industrious life" (l. 437).

This sort of subject matter could be dull enough; it provided material for many "set piece" descriptions in well-forgotten eighteenth-century poems. And *Rural Sports* has its dull stretches. That these do not dominate the poem is due to the peculiar complexity of Gay's vision, manifested in his close attention to language. For an example, let us examine the uses of the word *air* within a comparatively short section of the poem. In line 111, "Millions of worlds hang in the spacious air." Later comes a metaphoric couplet: "So the gay lady, with expensive care,/Borrows the pride of land, of sea, and air" (ll. 187-88). A few lines after: "The scaly shoals float by, and seiz'd with fear/Behold their fellows tost in thinner air" (ll. 217-18). Then the fish, drawn to shore, "lifts his nostrils in the sick'ning air" (l. 250); and, finally for our purposes, when Gay turns to hunting he describes the greyhound pursuing the hare and observes that the outwitted dog "snaps deceitful air with empty jaws" (l. 293).

It becomes obvious, looking at these excerpts in conjunction with one another, that Gay speaks of air each time in a radically different sense. Each individual sense, moreover, is fairly complicated in itself. The line about "millions of worlds" provides a momentary God's-eye-view of the universe. Its poetic effect depends first on the word *hang*, implicitly reminiscent of the Miltonic vision of the world suspended by a golden chain from heaven, but expanding that vision. "Spacious air" is also vital to the line, with its suggestion that infinite space can be perceived as a comfortable rather than as a frightening fact. The universe suggested is an ordered one, and the poet's joy at that fact is apparent.

How different is the vision of air implied by the gay lady's borrowing from it. By the conjunction of land, sea, and air, we are reminded faintly once more of the ordered universe—but reminded also of the sense in which human pride and vanity substitute a frivolous for a cosmic order. Land, sea, and air are for the lady essentially differentiated not at all; all merely gratify vanity, and the universe previously implicitly perceived as dominated by heaven is now reduced to a tiny system revolving around a single bedizened belle.

In the next reference, we move even farther from a divine perspective—to the fishes' view, in which water is the true air and the air which human beings breathe is frightening because "thinner." Its frightening quality is more explicit when it becomes "the sick'ning air": the element of death to a fish although of life to a man. And the dog's point of view makes it "deceitful" because of its very emptiness: air is now important because of what it does *not* contain, at a given spot in a given moment, rather than because of what it *does* contain ("millions of worlds").

We have been given, then, five different ways of considering air, all of which rely on various human preconceptions—if only to reverse or to expand them. Each attitude toward air is interesting in itself; each is appropriate to its moment in the poem. But the attitudes are even more revealing in relation to one another. The gay lady's perspective becomes more significant because we have previously been reminded of a more inclusive, more important way of looking at our natural environment; the fishes' point of view, with its reversal of the human, carries subtle ironic force when we have been reminded of the possibility that normal standards can be reversed, or seriously limited, even within the human world. For the fish and for the dog, air is significant in what it lacks (life-giving water, rabbits to kill); for the human being it is important in what it offers, but what it offers can be perceived in many different ways (as the element of life, the stuff of vanity, objects for philosophic contemplation). Gay has, in effect, put all these attitudes side by side. We discover through them that the concerns of a poem of limited theme have widened a good deal.

Of course, normally we do not consider such curious conjunctions of meaning, for *Rural Sports* does not insist on them; certainly the reader would not ordinarily work out these implications in such detail. Yet the effect of expansion can operate even without conscious recognition of it, by the sheer power of repeated instances. These references to air are by no means the only examples of Gay's technique of placing different uses of a word side by side for consideration. Some instances are more obvious than others, but the cumulative effect is inescapable. If we are told about birds that "death in thunder overtakes their flight" (1. 342)—an economical way of suggesting the extent to which the arbitrary intervention of man in the animal world must seem to the animals themselves merely one more inexplicable natural phenomenon: thunder or guns, it's all the same—a few lines later we learn that "The jocund thunder wakes th' enliven'd hounds" (1. 368). In this case, the thunder is that of the huntsman's horn, welcomed by the dogs but the signal of potential destruction to the game. The earlier use of the word must influence the later; we are reminded once more of the importance of point of view: the extent to which (and this is a minor but meaningful theme of the hunting passages) one's attitude toward hunting must depend upon whether one is hunter or hunted. Similarly, we hear about the "subtle hare" (1. 294), and then, a bit later, about the "subtle dog" (1. 309). Both animals are equally skillful, equally sagacious, to use one of Gay's own words, but their modes of cleverness are opposed: the result of subtlety in the dog must inevitably be the destruction of the hare in all its subtlety.

The ultimate effect of repeated variations of this sort is not merely to convince us that Gay is sympathetic to animals. It is rather to suggest a breadth of perspective vital to *Rural Sports*. Speaking of the hunting of larks, Gay explains that the birds are enticed to come near the ground by rays of light reflected from a "twinkling glass." He summarizes,

> Pride lures the little warbler from the skies:
> The light-enamour'd bird deluded dies.
> (11. 360-61)

This statement may recall the earlier description of "female pride" (1. 178), the gay lady who "Borrows the pride of land, of sea, and air" until she becomes merely a "glittering thing" (1. 189). Her pride consists in her unwillingness to accept her natural state; by failing to be properly herself, trying to be more, to plunder the universe for the sake of her vanity, she reduces herself below the level of humanity to that of mere "thingness." Similarly, the bird leaves his proper station, rejects the light of the skies, to come down to earth for a lesser gleam, enamored of light as the lady is of "Furs, pearls, and plumes." As a result he dies; the lady is more deviously destroyed.

The connection between lady and bird is implicit not merely in the word *pride*, but also in the concepts invoked. The question of perspective here becomes particularly important. Gay sees the bird from the same point of view as that with which he contemplates ladies, and the lady with the same eye he turns on birds. At his best, he manages to make this poem, in its consideration of merely rural concerns, significantly concerned also with the central problems of life. Judgment and skill, hope and fear, treachery and faithfulness are involved in these sporting affairs as in more important ones, and Gay usually remembers this fact. Hunting is not seen as an image of human life; rather, the poet's consciousness of a broader scheme of judgment, a broader realm of affairs, informs his treatment of comparatively trivial concerns.

In the best passages of *Rural Sports*, however, there is no indication that the poet considers country pursuits trivial and city ones important, and no clear indication of the reverse system of values. When he speaks of fly fishing, Gay mentions the necessity of making the flies in such a way "That nature seems to live again in art" (1. 208). His vision of the actual occupation of fishing is of moments in which "all thy hope hangs on a single hair" (1. 210). Both these statements, although they have perfectly literal force in the context, suggest also an expanded area of reference and invite the reader to make connections to other realms of experience. Gay's characteristic method, in short, is that of expansion: he places ideas, insights, words into meaningful conjunctions, implicit or explicit.

It is a method quite different from that of Virgil. Far more consistently and more forcefully than *Rural Sports*, the *Georgics*, with *work* as their subject, insist that each detail is more meaningful than the nominal subject matter (the concerns of the farmer) would suggest. But Virgil conveys significance primarily through *deepening* rather than expanding. Bees and horses and bulls are important, ultimately as well as initially, as beings *in themselves*—not as analogues for human problems. Their importance, to be sure, derives largely from the fact that Virgil perceives them so clearly in their proper roles in the cosmic scheme of things. He deals always with a hierarchical universe. Perceiving clearly a cosmos in which the gods have their place, man has his, cows theirs, he realizes intensely the ultimate importance of each individual participant in the total scheme. If his discussion of bees, for example, leads one to feel that the lives of the bees have lessons for men, it is only because the bees are fulfilling their functions with perfect propriety, perfect order; and one is made conscious of the fact that man does not always function with equal order and propriety. The total scheme, with its ultimately supernatural sanctions, is always implicit in each individual observation.

Gay, on the other hand, although he is capable, as we have seen, of making reference to a cosmic scheme, is not predominantly conscious of any particular system of order. His perspective varies, and its variations are themselves important; moreover, breadth of perspective provides a technique for redeeming the apparent triviality of sports—play—as a subject. One of Gay's favorite methods of "broadening" is to suggest the contrary-to-fact, the technique that Keats employed so brilliantly in, for example, "La Belle Dame Sans Merci":

> The sedge is withered from the lake,
> And no birds sing

—which suggests simultaneously the bleak present and the more luxuriant past. Gay uses the device so frequently that it becomes a dominant mannerism. "No warbling cheers the woods" (1. 95); "no rude gale disturbs the sleeping trees" (1. 97); "No swelling inundation hides the grounds" (1. 125); the rapid surface of the brook is "unknown to weeds" (1. 142); the bosom of the fisherman "glows with treasures yet uncaught" (1. 146). And so on, particularly in the first canto of the poem. The actual fact and its hypothetical opposite are suggested at once; Gay reminds us repeatedly that he is aware of contradictory possibilities. And when he convincingly evokes the sense of these possibilities, *Rural Sports* is most successful.

But the poem is not, as a whole, so successful as these comments may suggest. If Gay occasionally manages to infuse his Virgilian imitation with a truly felt personal vision, more often his insights seem uncontrolled, his verbal conjunctions random collocations of meaning rather than significant, selected juxtapositions. Toward the end of the poem, Gay offers a fairly lengthy treatment of the lot of the rural maid:

> What happiness the rural maid attends,
> In cheerful labour while each day she spends!
> She gratefully receives what heav'n has sent,
> And, rich in poverty, enjoys content.
> (11. 410-13)

The paradox ("rich in poverty") is all too easy, but the passage continues to yet more distasteful sentimentalities, as it systematically contrasts the lot of the country maiden with that of the "courtly dame." The advantage is all on the side of the country girl, who is neither hypochondriac nor melancholy, who never yearns for "glaring equipage," who does not carelessly lose her reputation or wear out her beauty at midnight masquerades. "If love's soft passion in her bosom reign," Gay observes comfortably, "An equal passion warms her happy swain" (11. 426-27). The explicit comparison between rural and urban values finds all good in the country, all evil in the town; the poet can come to such conclusions only by insistent dwelling on the superficial. His is a determined refusal to look beneath the surface.

That Gay was capable of looking beneath surfaces the rest of the poem frequently suggests. But that he was capable of rejecting his own insights is perhaps ultimately more significant. The convention of rural bliss was as readily available to him as that of civilized sophistication, and he chose to rely on it as an easy resolution to his poem. One is reminded of Rasselas's sister, in Dr. Johnson's moral fable: after discovering that shepherds are in actuality brutish, stupid, and malicious, she yet remains unaccountably convinced that true bliss is to be found in the pastoral life; she and some selected maiden friends will tend their sheep in luxuriant grasslands forever free from storms, indulging the while in the pleasures of polite conversation.

Gay retreats from reality in a similar fashion at the end of *Rural Sports;* he prefers the country to the town not for genuine reasons, as he did at the beginning of the poem, but for illusory ones. And the reader is thus caused to wonder about the integrity of the piece as a whole. The breadth of perspective which the poem offers, potentially valuable as a source of complexity, may be, after all, merely a mode of avoiding commitment. The brilliant patterns of language, economy of sentence structure, pieces of perfect selectivity do not add up to anything richly coherent or totally meaningful. The verdict finally on *Rural Sports* must be that it offers instance after instance of genuine poetic power and skill, that it is clearly the work of a man capable of being a poet—but also of a man who had not yet found his proper subject and mode, who sometimes unfortunately relied on fashionable convention rather than on honest feeling.

III

With *The Fan,* his next published poem, Gay came no closer to finding his own subject matter and tone—indeed, he moved farther away from his true note. A long poem containing a series of Ovidian episodes in a pseudo-mythological framework, *The Fan* seems now unutterably trivial and almost unreadable. "I am very much recreated and refreshed with the News of the advancement of the *Fan,*" wrote Pope in August, 1713, "which I doubt not will delight the Eye and Sense of the Fair, as long as that agreeable Machine shall play in the Hands of Posterity. I am glad your *Fan* is mounted so soon, but I wou'd have you varnish and glaze it at your leisure, and polish the Sticks as much as you can." [3] Reading the poem, it is hard to tell whether Gay varnished and polished too little or too much. At any rate, *The Fan* suffers badly by comparison with *The Rape of the Lock,* written at approximately the same time, which deals infinitely more expertly with the concerns and values of polite society.

Gay's next literary endeavor was far more successful, by contemporary and by modern standards. *The Shepherd's Week* is still frequently anthologized, still thought to be essentially representative of its author, and still a subject for controversy. The success of the poem and its representative qualities are clearly related to the positive aspects of Gay's poetry that we have discovered in his earlier works; and the controversy points to some of the central problems in evaluating Gay as poet and as thinker.

The dispute over *The Shepherd's Week,* to outline it in the simplest terms, has to do with defining the literary traditions that Gay here employs and—more crucially—with understanding his attitudes toward them. The matter was not clear at the time of the poem's first publication; and, although it has been clarified to some extent in the two and a half centuries since that time, there is still room for question. The most strongly supported theory is the one with Pope's authority behind it: Gay wrote his pastorals to defend Pope and to attack Ambrose Philips.

The Pope-Philips quarrel over the proper criteria for pastoral was one of the most famous and fierce literary disputes of the early part of the eighteenth century: it focuses for us the whole question of what traditions a poet should properly employ in writing about the country, and in what way it is proper for him to employ them. Philip's pastorals were published first in 1708; Pope's, in 1709; both later appeared in the same volume of Tonson's *Miscellany*. At the beginning, there was no opposition between the two men; indeed, Pope writes to his friend Henry Cromwell quite generously about his rival's verse, summing up: "In the whole, I agree with the Tatler, that we have no better Eclogs in our Language." [4] The trouble started over a series of essays which appeared in the *Guardian* in April, 1713.[5] Usually attributed to Thomas Tickell (although there is some possibility that they were written by Steele), these essays set up a series of criteria for pastoral poetry and illustrate excellence in the genre almost entirely by examples from Philips' pastorals, ignoring Pope. Angered by the omission, Pope submitted anonymously to the *Guardian* his own essay on pastoral, which purports to continue the praise of Philips by criticizing adversely the eclogues of Pope himself. The criticism is, of course, satiric; the paper (*Guardian* No. 40) makes Philips look ridiculous. Pope quotes, for example, some extraordinarily bad verses:

> Ah me the while! ah me! the luckless day,
> Ah luckless lad! the rather might I say;
> Ah silly I! more silly than my sheep,
> Which on the flowery plains I once did keep.

Then he comments, devastatingly: "How he still charms the ear with these artful repetitions of the epithets; and how significant is the last verse! I defy the most common reader to repeat them, without feeling some motions of compassion."

Gay was, of course, a friend and admirer of Pope's; and at this time he was much involved in the activities of Pope, Swift, and the Scriblerus Club. In a letter to John Caryll (June 8, 1714), Pope explains his annoyance with Philips on the grounds that Philips had held back subscription money actually due to Pope. He then says, quite explicitly, "It is to this management of *Philips*, that the world owes Mr. *Gay's Pastorals*."[6] Hoyt Trowbridge has demonstrated the extent to which Gay's poems may be taken as detailed parodies of Philips,' echoing point by point the criticisms of Philips implied by Pope's *Guardian* paper.[7] Pope objects to Philips' obsolete language, his use of undignified rustic names, his violations of decorum (as in the listing in conjunction of flowers that actually bloom only at different seasons of the year), his use of platitudinous proverbs, his pseudo-simplicity, and his inanity.[8] All these aspects of Philips' poetry are echoed by Gay; some are explicitly commented on in his ironic proem. Professor Trowbridge sums up by observing that Gay's "purpose is to reveal the artistic fatuity of Tickell's pastoral theory and of Philips' practice; . . . if, as Tickell claimed, the rules of pastoral were to be drawn from the practice of Philips, this was the sort of poem which must result. This idea, implicit in Gay's proem and consistently applied in the eclogues themselves, is the organizing principle of *The Shepherd's Week*. It is this idea which gives the poem a coherent artistic plan" (88).

This argument is both logical and convincing. But arguments of almost equal force have been presented for the theory that

Gay was actually satirizing Sir Richard Blackmore, that his central target was Thomas D'Urfey, and that he was really satirizing no one at all. Blackmore, a doctor who by his own confession composed his poems of interminable length in his head while doing his medical rounds, was a favorite target of early eighteenth-century wits. The very image of dullness, he was an obvious butt because of his self-importance, because of the extent to which he had won undeserved fame, and because his political and moral ideas were sharply opposed to those of Pope, Swift, and their circle. Most generally admired among Blackmore's works were his *Creation*, a long poem praising God through the wonders of His creation, and his "Song of Mopas," from *Prince Arthur*, which has a similar theme. John Robert Moore has shown how Blackmore's favorite structural devices and his important themes are systematically parodied in "Saturday," the final poem of *The Shepherd's Week*.[9] And here, too, the evidence is impressive and the suggested connections illuminating. The same might be said of the demonstration by William D. Ellis, Jr., that Gay may have wished to attack the popular song writer Thomas D'Urfey, who is explicitly mentioned in *The Shepherd's Week*.[10] Ellis points out that "ballad material, much like that for which D'Urfey gained his popularity," helped to supply the fable of three of Gay's eclogues" ("Tuesday," "Wednesday," and "Thursday") (211); that the members of the Scriblerus Club were concerned to attack D'Urfey (206-07); and that there are in "Saturday" explicit references to the song writer.

Yet critics who have recorded their admiration of *The Shepherd's Week* have tended to justify the poem not as a satiric work, but as a straightforward, accurate, and at times moving rendition of rural actuality. Thomas Purney, writing on pastoral as early as 1717, "believes that Gay gave a true picture 'of the Fellows and Wenches in the Country, and put down every thing' just as he 'observ'd them act.'"[11] Dr. Johnson, who records the history of the Pope-Philips controversy and Gay's share in it, concludes: "But the effect of reality and truth became conspicuous, even when the intention was to shew them groveling and degraded. These Pastorals became popular, and were read with delight, as just representations of rural manners and occupations, by those who had no interest in the rivalry of the poets, nor knowledge of the critical dispute."[12] And the recent volume on the early eighteenth century in the Oxford History of English Literature observes that *The Shepherd's Week* was Gay's "first durable contribution to the poetic canon," apparently mainly because in the poem Gay "is firmly contemporary and realistic."[13]

These theories, to be sure, are not really incompatible with one another. It is quite probable that Gay began writing his pastorals in the service of the Pope-Philips dispute; that he included with the satire of Philips some digs at that even more vulnerable pastoral poet, D'Urfey; that the satire on Blackmore was incidental; and that, in spite of all these satiric purposes, the poem rests on a firm foundation of clearly perceived and precisely rendered actuality. This explanation is probable not only because each critical theory seems individually convincing, but because Gay in his early poetry wavered so conspicuously among various perspectives, searched several literary traditions, and incorporated as many points of view as he conceivably could in, for example, *Rural Sports*. The existence of widely divergent explanations of the origin and effect of *The Shepherd's Week* is critically significant as well as historically interesting: it suggests once more the extent to which Gay achieved poetic effects not merely by imitating a model but by bringing traditional material into meaningful conjunction with quite different systems of values. That *The Shepherd's Week* is so much more successful than *Rural Sports* may be partly explained by the fact that in it the conjunctions seem systematically controlled and ultimately purposeful.

The Shepherd's Week presents an image of rural life radically different from that at the end of *Rural Sports*, but one in the long run more appealing. Five of the six eclogues concern love, traditional subject for pastoral, with frequent verbal parody-echoes of Virgil pointed out by Gay's own notes. (William Henry Irving, indeed, believes that in the beginning the poem was intended as "burlesque of Vergil rather than ridicule of Philips."[14]) Gay's maidens are of quite a different sort from Virgil's; this was, after all, an important point of the joke. "Thou wilt not find my shepherdesses idly piping on oaten reeds," Gay writes in his proem, "but milking the kine, tying up the sheaves, or if the hogs are astray driving them to their styes."[15] He presents the notion of working shepherdesses as a jest, implicitly inviting his readers to recall the girls in Virgil's pastorals, who do nothing more serious than pelt their swains with apples; inviting them also to perceive how ridiculous were Philips' attempts to bring realism to the superbly artificial form of the pastoral. Yet, when Gay combines these two contradictory concepts of art, the result is frequently not ridiculous at all.

The idea of work is of primary importance in these poems, and not merely as a joke. As the shepherds in the first eclogue contend in praising their mistresses, each points out that his beloved makes toil sweeter, so that with her near, "Ev'n noon-tide labour seem'd an holiday" (1. 66). Cloddipole, who is to judge between them, finally refuses to make a choice—not, like the judge in Virgil's third eclogue, because the contestants are too equal, but because the time for singing and for playing at judgment is past:

> But see the sun-beams bright to labour warn,
> And gild the thatch of goodman *Hodges'* barn,
> Your herds for want of water stand adry,
> They're weary of your songs—and so am I.
> (11. 121-24)

The really meaningful context for action and for judgment throughout these pastorals is that of pastoral responsibility: the sun warns the swains to labor; the proper activity for shepherds is tending their sheep. Gay does not present his shepherds and shepherdesses milking the kine *instead of* idly piping, as he promises in the proem: the point is rather that he first shows them piping and singing, and then offers country work as a more meaningful alternative.

Similarly, in the second eclogue, "Tuesday, or, The Ditty," the result of Marian's unrequited love for Colin Clout is the loss of her ability to work well. She is, before Colin turns his affections elsewhere, the ideal country maiden—ideal, like Blouzelinda in "Friday," because responsible and expert at her work. But as a result of love the maid becomes "witless" (1. 17), and this adjective is not casually employed. Such terms as *witless* and *silly* are used frequently throughout these pastorals; almost invariably they point to genuine value judgments. Marian complains:

> Ah! woful day! ah, woful noon and morn!
> When first by thee my younglings white were shorn,
> Then first, I ween, I cast a lover's eye,
> My sheep were silly, but more silly I.
> (11. 25-28)

This is obviously a parody of the same passage from Philips that Pope had chosen to make fun of. But it is more than parody. Philips' swain utters a perfectly conventional complaint, ludicrously unaware of its literal force. Marian's complaint, on the other hand, is a genuine commentary on the destruction of personal value involved in giving up "all busy heed." The context in which she recognizes her silliness is that of sheep shearing (compare Philips' vision of sheep browsing "flowery plains"), and the judgment she makes of herself is perfectly accurate: it is also Gay's judgment. But it is not inevitable: Gay does not suggest that the country maiden *must* be as silly as her sheep. On the contrary, "Tuesday" systematically sets up a series of contrasts between present and past which establish a vision of the rural ideal quite different from the romantic one of *Rural Sports.* Marian asserts her own superiority to Colin Clout's other sweetheart on the grounds that she is willing to work harder for Colin's sake; she recollects the glories of the past (11. 49-72) in terms of shared work. The poem is resolved with a ludicrously matter-of-fact image:

> Thus *Marian* wail'd, her eyes with tears brimfull,
> When Goody *Dobbins* brought her cow to bull.
> With apron blue to dry her tears she sought,
> Then saw the cow well serv'd, and took a groat.
> (11. 103-36)

Sven Armens comments on this passage, "The necessity of fulfilling her daily tasks does afford some release for her grief-stricken existence. . . . Love is only a part of her life. When it vanishes, the country maid has something else of value left, a useful role as a contributing member of her society."[16] This analysis fails to point out that the "useful role" is partly a joke: the cow-bull episode places matters of love in a new perspective. "Friday," the dirge for Blouzelinda, ends with the grief-stricken shepherds consoling themselves for the loss of one maiden by finding another; "Thursday," the complaint and spellcasting of lovelorn Hobnelia, is resolved by the quite effortless seduction of the girl. Love and sex are, in this world, much the same; relations between men and women bear a conspicuous resemblance to those between cow and bull.

A reader may have ambivalent feelings about this fact. On the one hand, he is invited to look at these youths and maidens from the superior perspective of civilized sophistication, to laugh at them because of *their* conspicuous lack of sophistication—and, for that matter, even of civilization. But there is also the implicit juxtaposition of these country characters with the more romantically conceived ones of traditional Virgilian pastoral, and the advantage in this comparison is partly on the side of Gay's characters. If they are uncouth, they recognize and accept what they are; inasmuch as they are men and women of integrity, they are not ultimately comic.

In reading these poems we can never afford to be unaware that the comedy may turn at any moment back upon the reader. The worldly reader may laugh at these characters, but they might as readily laugh at him: they are more honest than he. The view of "civilized" life which Gay offers in *Trivia,* the fables, and the town eclogues frequently reminds us that beneath the facade of civilization men and women often resemble bulls and cows as much in the city as in the country; the difference is that in the city they ignore rather than accept the realities of mating animals.

The realism of the country is heavily stressed throughout *The Shepherd's Week.* In "Wednesday, or The Dumps," Sparabella, mourning her lost lover, decides finally to commit suicide. She is deterred, however, by her vanity:

> This penknife keen my windpipe shall divide.
> What, shall I fall as squeaking pigs have dy'd!
> No—to some tree this carcass I'll suspend.
> But worrying curs find such untimely end! . . .
> (11. 101-14)

Finally she decides to throw herself in the lake, "if courage holds" (1. 111); but by this time it is nightfall:

> The prudent maiden deems it now too late,
> And 'till to-morrow comes defers her fate.
> (11. 119-20)

The comedy here derives from the disproportion between the girl's exaggerated and romanticized sense of tragedy and her underlying realism, which makes her find constant excuses for deferring her fate, and which will obviously always prevent a dramatic denouement for her situation. But again, the comedy cuts two ways. We laugh at the maiden because she does *not* commit suicide; we would not laugh at her if she actually did kill herself. We are all too willing to accept seriously the posturings of sentimental self-dramatization. If Sparabella is ridiculous because of the gap between her image of herself and the actuality, more sophisticated readers may be equally ridiculous in their willingness to accept romantic poses as adequate bases for structuring actuality.

"Friday, or, The Dirge," also depends heavily on the tension between reality and romantic illusion. It is in some ways a genuinely moving dirge; it has moments of sharp perception and true feeling. Blouzelinda is mourned not as an idealized creature but as a girl who worked honestly and well, and for whom love was part of the natural pattern of life. At one point a mourning shepherd in conventional fashion invites nature to mourn her loss—yet his plea is not quite conventional after all.

> Henceforth the morn shall dewy sorrow shed,
> And ev'ning tears upon the grass be spread;
> The rolling streams with wat'ry grief shall flow,
> And winds shall moan aloud—when loud they blow.
> Henceforth, as oft as autumn shall return,
> The dropping trees, whene'er it rains, shall mourn;
> This season quite shall strip the country's pride,
> For 'twas in autumn *Blouzelinda* died.
>
> (11. 33-40)

These lines, which broadly parody common pastoral convention, also sum up the shepherd's real perception. Even in his grief, he has not lost sight of natural realities: he does not allow himself to believe that the normal order can be distorted as a result of one human death. Nothing will change except the interpretation of events. The dew that normally falls in the morning and evening, the streams that normally flow, the wind that blows and the trees that drip—all can now be explained in a different way; but the facts themselves have in no way been altered. The eclogue begins with Bumkinet's evocation of the bleakness of autumn, before he has learned of Blouzelinda's death; he can thus comment, "Yet e'en this season pleasance blithe affords" (1. 7). The same Bumkinet speaks later of the mourning of nature: only his perspective is different. To be sure, toward the end of his dirge he invites the fields to show "rueful symptoms" by substituting weeds for flowers as an emblem of the loss of beauty in Blouzelinda's death (11. 83-88), but this momentary comic deviation from realism (in a passage, incidentally, closely imitated from Virgil) is immediately compensated for by Bumkinet's matter-of-fact adjuration to the swains to make sure that they spell properly the inscription on Blouzelinda's gravestone.

The inscription itself, with its reminder that "flesh is grass," (1. 92) is of central importance not only to this eclogue but to the entire series. It works in two ways: it insists on the ultimate unimportance of the lives of these people, in all their transience; but also it insists that human life participates meaningfully in the natural cycle. Flesh quite literally becomes grass which is eaten by cows which must be tended by yet other human beings; at every point in the cycle, man is directly involved with nature, and his acceptance of his responsibilities is also an acceptance of his place in the natural order. So Blouzelinda on her deathbed worries about the welfare of her poultry and her calf; so the mourners at her grave are conscious of the fact that the preacher talks somewhat too long, and they retreat from mourning to cider, because "Excessive sorrow is exceeding dry" (1. 152). The point is not merely that these are insensitive country bumpkins, although we are indeed from time to time invited to think so; it is also that these particular sorts of insensitivity imply the recognition that sentimentality over the dead is not so important as the duties—and even the pleasures—of the living.

But surely Gay would laugh at so heavy-handed and serious a treatment of his shepherds and shepherdesses, who retain their vividness finally as a result of their charm. When Cuddy describes his Buxoma as

> Clean as young lambkins or the goose's down,
> And like the goldfinch in her Sunday gown
> ("Monday," 11. 51-52),

he provides a strong poetic evocation of her appeal; when dismal Sparabella cries out,

> Sooner shall scriech-owls bask in sunny day,
> And the slow ass on trees, like squirrels, play, . . .
> Than I forget my shepherd's wonted love
> ("Wednesday," 11. 69-70,72),

we enjoy her imagery although we may not altogether accept her grief.

The charm of these characters is far more important than any philosophical significance we may posit for them. But what is its ultimate effect? Professor Trowbridge comments on this point: "Like Shakespeare's artisans, shepherds, and squires, Gay's rustics have a certain naïve charm, but from the sophisticated urban point of view which Gay (like Shakespeare) expected in his readers, these dairymaids and swineherds are ludicrous—delightful but absurd." [17] But the matter is more complicated. If Gay really mocks Philips and D'Urfey and Blackmore and Virgil, while he conveys directly and convincingly the actualities of country existence—if he does all these things successfully, his effects must be extraordinarily various. Surely he can simultaneously deride Philips' "realism" and Virgil's artifice, Blackmore's pretentiousness and D'Urfey's rusticity, only by choosing for himself some middle position. That hypothetical midway norm is never directly embodied in the poem, but it is implicit; and it allows Gay to criticize the city through the demonstrated standards of the country, inasmuch as these standards involve real values, as well as to criticize the country by the implicit standards of the city. He pretends, as Professor Trowbridge points out, to assume "the character and attitudes of a rustic bard" (86), and he does so in order to mock the rustic bard. Yet he uses his persona also as a convenience for exposing the genuine values that the country has to offer. The pure nostalgia which dominates and frequently weakens *Rural Sports* has here been combined with the sophistication which unsuccessfully seeks to find expression in *The Fan;* the skill at parodying conventional forms while expressing personal perceptions through them which we noted even in *Wine* has now found more appropriate subject matter. And the complexity which makes *The Shepherd's Week* interesting seems a direct product of the tension between the point of view of the country man and the more fashionable perspective which contradicts it, both points of view incorporated in the poet. Gay has here found a mask which does not entirely obscure his own features: uncomfortable in the total guise of sophisticate, unwilling to commit himself completely to the unfashionable posture of a lover of the country, he adapts many voices to his own use. Mocking Ambrose Philips, imitating Virgil, parodying the unrealistic conventions of pastoral, he seems for the first time to have succeeded in saying what he wanted to say. Later in his poetic career he would want to say more—and then, too, his problem would be to find the proper voice with which to say it.

CHAPTER 2

Trivia

TRIVIA (1716) did for the town what *The Shepherd's Week* had done for the country. By the time it was published Gay himself had become more firmly committed to London. He was by then an established member—indeed, the secretary—of the Scriblerus Club, which existed to mock pretension and pedantry. Its members included Pope, Swift, Parnell, and Dr. Arbuthnot, all experts at satire. All helped Gay gather subscriptions for *Trivia,* as they had earlier helped him to brief political preferment (he was secretary to Lord Clarendon on a mission to Hanover, but the expedition and the appointment were ended abruptly by Queen Anne's death) and had encouraged him to write praises of royalty in order to win some new office. He was, as he had wished to be, a member of the best literary society; if he had to worry about opportunities for advancement, at least he need worry no longer that he might be destined for a mercer. Yet his sense of tension clearly persisted: he had not committed himself to a single point of view. *The Shepherd's Week* had expressed his ambiguous feelings about the country life he had abandoned, and *Trivia* conveys a similar sense of ambiguity about the city life he had chosen.

William Henry Irving, Gay's most recent biographer, says without qualification that *Trivia* is the greatest poem in English on London life.[1] Its accomplishment is not merely to describe but to make description convey perception, to enliven the city through poetic insight. When Gay remarks, speaking of spring, that "all the *Mall* in leafy ruin lies" (Bk. I, 1. 27), he provides a brilliant image of nature turning to chaos the orderliness of civilization. The point of view from which leaves represent ruin is simultaneously evoked and mocked: we are reminded of the difference between the perspective of the country and that of the city. Yet the difference in perspective in no way affects the salient fact that nature can dominate and create beauty in the city as in the country.

Gay's images of beauty, however, are not all of *natural* beauty. Here is a more extended evocation of the Mall:

> The ladies gayly dress'd, the *Mall* adorn
> With various dyes, and paint the sunny morn;
> The wanton fawns with frisking pleasure range,
> And chirping sparrows greet the welcome change:
> Not that their minds with greater skill are fraught,
> Endu'd by instinct, or by reason taught,
> The seasons operate on ev'ry breast;
> 'Tis hence that fawns are brisk, and ladies drest.
> (Bk. I, 11. 145-52)

The final couplet has a Popean wit of structure, but no Popean bite; indeed, the entire passage is singularly free of venom. We would expect Gay to be sharply critical of ladies for "painting": makeup was an obvious target for satire. But in fact, though the ladies may be subtly criticized for being no *more* than fawns or sparrows, there is certainly no implication that they are any *less* charming. Toward fawns and ladies alike Gay preserves precisely the same tone of affectionate delight. Sparrows chirp, fawns are brisk, ladies bring out their spring finery for the same reasons; all these activities are equally subrational reactions to the change of seasons. Visually, the scene is brilliant in its very indistinctness, like an impressionist painting. The ladies exist merely to "adorn" the Mall; they are vividly artificial. The coming of spring makes them react in ways analogical to those of the animals, but the animals are also analogues for the women: "wantonness" (in its most innocent and fawnlike sense), "frisking," and "chirping" are as characteristic feminine activities as animal ones. The poet's perceptions are first of all visual: he sees all participants in the scene as essentially decorative, as helping to "paint the sunny morn." Yet the visual perception implies a more profound vision, of the way in which, whether in city or in country, all members of the Great Chain of Being participate in the same pattern of order and beauty.

Of course not all Gay's perceptions are of beauty. He offers a much more specific image of the London whore than of the

London lady; again, his precise description implies moral as well as physical vision.

> 'Tis she who nightly strowls with saunt'ring pace,
> No stubborn stays her yielding shape embrace;
> Beneath the lamp her tawdry ribbons glare,
> The new-scower'd manteau, and the slattern air;
> High-draggled petticoats her travels show,
> And hollow cheeks with artful blushes glow;
> With flatt'ring sounds she soothes the cred'lous ear,
> My noble captain! charmer! love! my dear!
> In riding-hood near tavern-doors she plies,
> Or muffled pinners hide her livid eyes. . . .
> (Bk. III, 11. 267-76)

A number of Gay's most characteristic techniques are demonstrated here. The second line of the passage, for example, has the sort of richness of implication peculiar to eighteenth-century poetry at its best. The terms applied to the woman's clothes and figure are equally applicable to her nature and profession. The line is framed by the sort of negative suggestion we examined in *Rural Sports;* here it suggests simultaneously the sordid reality and its hypothetical, unrealized alternative: the woman who would not be "yielding," either in physical softness, voluptuousness, or in its moral equivalent. Moreover, the form of the sentence helps to place significant emphasis upon its final word: no *stays* embrace this yielding shape; what (or who), then, *does* embrace it? Indeed, the whole effect of the line depends upon the number of alternatives it suggests through the ambiguity of its terminology: the "stubbornness" which stays a woman from yielding, or that which stays her from social conformity; the woman who yields, the woman who does not; the woman who is embraced by stays, for purposes of restraint, or one who is embraced by men, for dissipation; or one who needs neither men nor stays, but is "unyielding" in herself. In the context of such alternatives, the harlot gains significance.

Not every line, to be sure, is so tightly packed; but virtually every line reinforces the implications of this one through relying, like it, on expansion of implication. The prostitute's ribbons "glare" and her cheeks "glow," both shedding the lurid false light which is one of Gay's characteristic symbols of corruption. (The denunciation of wealth, at the end of Book II, uses "glaring," "bright," "glows," and "flames," all within ten lines, to evoke the deceptive, destructive brilliance of the rich.) This light reveals its falsity by its conjunction with many images of dirt and sordidness: the ribbons which glare are also "tawdry"; the whore's petticoats are "draggled," her cheeks hollow, her eyes livid. The simple contrast between the "new-scower'd manteau" and the "slattern air" becomes more complicated as we realize that all the apparently positive aspects of this woman (the cleanliness of her coat, the glow of her cheeks, the soothing gentleness of her speech) are deliberate attempts to deceive. Only the credulous could be so deceived, but even the sophisticated must be made to understand the full sordidness of this mode of deception.

These examples suggest how misleading is the praise of those who find in *Trivia* primarily an accurate evocation of, a conveniently versified guide to, London as it actually was in the early eighteenth century. The poem pretends to be no more than this; but the important fact about the descriptions is not that they evoke physical reality: physical evocation here conveys moral as well as aesthetic judgment. Sometimes Gay achieves visionary brilliance in a flash, in a pair of words, or a single word, as when he speaks of the fop whose coat is "spatter'd o'er with lace" (I, 1. 54). The word *spatter'd* conveys a wonderful scorn in its visual clarity: lace on this coat is like mud. Or, more conventionally, "in the doubtful day the woodcock flies" (I, 1. 234): *doubtful* provides an image of the early morning, the dividing line between night and day, and suggests that every early morning is necessarily a time of doubt, when one does not know what the day is to bring. (This second meaning is particularly appropriate in the context: this is the day on which Vulcan is to spy Patty, in the pseudo-mythological tale of the invention of pattens.) Always, when Gay's description is at its most vivid and evocative, it gains value not merely from precision of physical observation but also from accompanying moral insight.

II

Not all the moral judgments of *Trivia,* obviously, are implied by the description. Gay also reveals directly that his system of values for judging the city is much the same as the standards by which he judged the country. Honesty, hard work, practicality were praised in the youths and maidens of *The Shepherd's Week;* they are also central virtues in *Trivia.*

> Let beaus their canes with amber tipt produce,
> Be theirs for empty show, but thine for use.
> In gilded chariots while they loll at ease,
> And lazily insure a life disease;
> While softer chairs the tawdry load convey
> To Court, to White's, assemblies, or the Play;
> Rosie-complexion'd health thy steps attends,
> And exercise thy lasting youth defends.
> (I, 67-74)

The reduction of a bevy of fine ladies to "the tawdry load" is marvelously condescending, and the same note of scorn toward the lazy, the useless, the riders in carriages, sounds again and again. The walker provides an image of energy, health, and purpose which contrasts with the effeteness, illness, and essential purposelessness of the riders. Sven Armens comments on the consistent association of walking with poverty and virtue, riding with wealth and evil;[2] it is certainly true that the evil which early in the poem is defined simply as the absence of the good qualities possessed by the walker is gradually more fully defined through images of fraud, greed, and exploitation associated with the wealthy. But Gay recognizes the possibility of corruption in walkers as well as in riders: he does not rely on merely automatic association between walking and goodness. Although he says, "For you, O honest men, these useful lays/ The muse prepares" (I, 119-20), he sometimes seems to doubt the essential virtue of those he directly addresses. The poem is, after all, didactic—and only partly a joke. "You," the reader, are always in the action, as a reminder that *Trivia* is designed to teach the skills of city living. These skills, although they may be dismissed as merely "trivial," are also modes of discipline and moral insight; inasmuch as the city tends to corrupt, moral insight is desperately needed. Consider Gay's attitude in this passage nominally devoted to condemnation of the poor young thief:

Where the mob gathers, swiftly shoot along,
Nor idly mingle in the noisy throng.
Lur'd by the silver hilt, amid the swarm,
The subtil artist will thy side disarm.
Nor is thy flaxen wigg with safety worn;
High on the shoulder, in a basket borne,
Lurks the sly boy; whose hand to rapine bred,
Plucks off the curling honours of thy head.
Here dives the skulking thief with practis'd slight,
And unfelt fingers make thy pocket light.
Where's now thy watch, with all its trinkets, flown?
And thy late snuff-box is no more thy own.
But lo! his bolder theft some tradesman spies,
Swift from his prey the scudding lurcher flies;
Dext'rous he 'scapes the coach with nimble bounds,
Whilst ev'ry honest tongue "*stop thief*" resounds.
So speeds the wily fox, alarm'd by fear,
Who lately filch'd the turkey's callow care;
Hounds following hounds grow louder as he flies,
And injur'd tenants join the hunter's cries.
Breathless he stumbling falls: Ill-fated boy!
Why did not honest work thy youth employ?
(III, 51-72)

The point of view of the poet in this passage is by no means identical with that of the hypothetical victim of the robbery, the "you" of the poem. For one thing, Gay does not take material possessions entirely seriously. The tone of "Where's now thy watch, with all its trinkets, flown?" is hardly sympathetic. Similarly, "thy late snuff-box," structurally analogous to the more common locution of "the late Mr. X," hints ironically that the possessor of snuff boxes is all too likely to give them an excessive importance. In this context "the curling honours of thy head," for the walker's wig, becomes more than common eighteenth-century periphrasis or circumlocution: it suggests once more the undue significance which gentlemen accord to superficial images of respectability or prestige.

If the comments on the victim have overtones of satiric disapproval, the descriptions of the thief are equally ambiguous. He is characterized—ironically, to be sure—as the "subtil artist." His hand is "to rapine bred": the latinate term, like the description of the boy as an "artist," reminds us that language and attitude can dignify thieves as easily as wigs. He uses "practis'd slight" in his stealing; he is "dext'rous" in escaping the coach. Although such terms as "skulking thief" and "scudding lurcher" (*lurcher:* one who watches to pilfer, or to betray or entrap) suggest the poet's disapproval, the passage also hints a paradoxical admiration for the boy's skill in his despicable profession.

The ambiguities of attitude here are summed up by the long concluding mock-epic simile. Gay was in his *Fables* to make more extensive use of comparisons between human beings and animals; some of the potential complexity of the device is suggested here. The simile seems to emphasize the boy's "badness" (the fox is, after all, the conventional folktale villain) and the comparative uprightness of his pursuers. Yet to be sympathetic to the hounds is not the only way of looking at a hunt. In *Rural Sports* Gay had earlier sympathized with animal victims; in this case, too, his sympathy is divided. The justification for pursuing the fox, as the simile is structured, is the fact that he has "filch'd the turkey's callow care." ("Callow," of course, in this case means young, unfledged.) The thievish boy, on the other hand, has stolen only a snuff box or a watch with its trinkets, which can be described as a "callow care" in quite another sense: the care only of someone who is himself callow (as in "callow youth"), unsophisticated, unknowledgeable about true values. Is the object of the pursuit really worth the chaos which the pursuit causes? "Injur'd tenants join the hunter's cries": the hunt, which has turned into a recreational activity, wantonly destroys the fields of the tenants. Gay does not dwell on the analogy, but he thus suggests the destruction of fruit stands and clothes stalls resulting from the tumultuous pursuit of a single ill-fated boy. Perhaps the cause does not justify the effect; the boy who seems at first equivalent to the wily fox comes to be more and more clearly a victim of society, until Gay's final moral question ("Why did not honest work thy youth employ?"), although it is partly parody, treating a small matter as though it were great, rings also with genuine pathos.

In the introduction to this passage, the walker is warned not to mingle idly in the noisy throng. The mishaps which may overtake him as the victim of thieves, are all, in Gay's eyes, the results of idleness: if he "swiftly shoots along," as the poet commands, he will not be robbed. The thief is sly, skulking—but he at least exercises skill; perhaps he merits more sympathy than the frivolous stroller. Gay values "honest work," of course, more than thievery; but he thinks the demonstration of skill, however meretricious, preferable to the failure to act meaningfully. "I find myself disquieted for want of having some pursuit; indolence & idleness are the most tiresome things in the world." [3] So Gay was to write to Swift; this horror of the idleness which constantly tempted him remained throughout his life. But one needs no biographical reference to perceive that in *Trivia* Gay considers idleness not merely an attribute of the rich (although a sense of their indolence is clearly at the heart of his condemnation), but a constant temptation of every man who is not actually forced by his economic position to work without ceasing. Certainly Gay condemns the thief, but he half-seriously values his skill and genuinely pities him; certainly he feels at least conventionally sorry for victims of robbery, but he also condemns them for the laxity which makes robbery convenient, and for the false sense of values which makes it profitable.

Meaningful work is the most strongly supported single value in the entire poem. Gay recognizes that "industry itself [must] submit to death" (II, 388), but the "itself" is significant: industry is, from his point of view (like Good Deeds in *Everyman*), a most unlikely victim of death because one of the highest of human virtues. He blames idleness for physical as well as moral ills:

> What, though no coach to frequent visit rolls,
> Nor for your shilling chairmen sling their poles;
> Yet still your nerves rheumatic pains defye,
> Nor lazy jaundice dulls your saffron eye;
> No wasting cough discharges sounds of death,
> Nor wheezing asthma heaves in vain for breath;
> Nor from your restless couch is heard the groan
> Of burning gout, or sedentary stone.
>
> (II, 503-10)

The words *lazy, sedentary,* and even, in this context, *wasting,* all used to describe diseases, emphasize the connection between idleness as cause and disease as effect. To have a "restless couch" becomes almost a positive characteristic: the man who is restless is at least protected from the temptation to commit the major sin of "lolling." In the passage immediately following the one quoted above, Gay recounts with glee the fate of the beau who, lolling in his gilded chariot to view with disdain the pedestrians that his coach spatters, is suddenly overturned and "disgraced" by the cart of a dustman. Idleness, as a central human evil, is inevitably attended by nemesis: this is the poem's constant assertion.

Indeed, for Gay walking the streets of London is not merely an "art" but a significant form of "work" in itself. He protects himself from the charge of exaggeration by his deprecatory tone, but an analogy he uses is revealing. Bookstalls, he explains, display to the passing walker their load of learning:

> Here, like the bee, that on industrious wing
> Collects the various odours of the spring,
> Walkers, at leisure, learning's flow'rs may spoil,
> Nor watch the wasting of the midnight oil. . . .
> (II, 555-58)

The irony here does not go very deep. The poet himself seems tempted by the combination of leisure and industry which walking offers, the opportunity to imitate the bee, that traditional model of the worker, without undue effort. Perhaps even more suggestive is another ironic passage which also cuts in two directions:

> Has not wise nature strung the legs and feet
> With firmest nerves, design'd to walk the street?
> Has she not given us hands, to groap aright,
> Amidst the frequent dangers of the night?
> And think'st thou not the double nostril meant,
> To warn from oily woes by previous scent?
> (III, 241-46)

This is an inverse statement of the point which Pope was to make so memorably in his *Essay on Man:*

> Why has not Man a microscopic eye?
> For this plain reason, Man is not a Fly.
> Say what the use, were finer optics given
> T'inspect a mite, not comprehend the heaven?
> (I, 193-96)

In both cases, the central idea is the same: that man has been given, by benevolent nature, precisely the qualities he needs to function in the world. Gay's explanation that the nose exists in order to warn us against oil which may, as he has pointed out slightly earlier, stain our coats is, of course, consciously ludicrous. But it also contains some essential truth. If his explanation of the value of legs and hands and noses is comically incomplete, it is valid as far as it goes; it is of a piece with the perception that walking the streets, which involves observation and judgment as well as recreation, has a meaningful place in the hierarchy of possible activities. A man fulfills certain human responsibilities through walking as Gay himself does and advocates: his walking, in this sense, is significantly human, as the fop's lolling is meaningfully anti-human in its denial of his obligation to use his faculties.

The laziness of fops is opposed to the industry of the lower classes; the pretensions of the fop, his high regard for appearances, is opposed to the pedestrian's concern for function. This theme is outlined early in the first book, in Gay's discussion of various sorts of coats. The poet rejects "the spoils of the Russian bear" (1. 50) as unfitting wear in town; likewise the various coats of the fop. Instead, he chooses a garment whose unsightliness is emphasized:

> That garment best the winter's rage defends,
> Which from the shoulders full and low depends;
> By various names in various counties known,
> Yet held in all the true *Surtout* alone,
> Be thine of *Kersey* firm, tho' small the cost,
> Then brave unwet the rain, unchill'd the frost.
> (I, 11. 55-60)

When, at the end of Book II, the poet cries, "O rather give me sweet content on foot,/Wrapt in my virtue, and a good surtout!" (11. 589-90), we realize that the connection between "virtue" and "surtout" is not merely accidental, nor is it just a joke; in a sense the wearing of a surtout, not beautiful but practical, is a visual demonstration of virtue.

Gay is constantly suspicious of appearances, eager to demonstrate the danger of relying on them:

> What walker shall his mean ambition fix
> On the false lustre of a coach and six?
> Let the vain virgin, lur'd by glaring show,
> Sigh for the liv'ries of th' embroider'd beau.
> (II, 569-72)

"False lustre" is ever visible in the town; one always risks being lured by glaring show. To walk the streets properly is partly an exercise in discrimination. One must discriminate, for example, between the false signs of the weather which superstition offers to "debase thy mind" (I, 187) and the true signs which careful observation provides to reveal the season or the day of the week. The observer who will think about what he sees gains practical advantages. The merely fashionable denizen of the town, incapable of perception, is hardly worth consideration. Gay misses no opportunity to underline his disgust with the principle of meaningless adornment. In the pseudo-mythological account of the origin of bootblacks, for example, occurs an incidental description of the prototype-bootblack's father:

> The muddy spots that dried upon his face,
> Like female patches, heighten'd ev'ry grace.
> (II, 119-20)

The simile works in two directions. Its joke, of course, is its mock-seriousness about the beauty of the scavenger's defects; mud is elevated to an adornment, incidentally satirizing female patches. If mud can be an unconscious adornment, consciously applied patches are no more intrinsically valuable. (This image is the converse and corollary of the earlier one envisioning the fop's coat "spatter'd o'er with lace.")

Or again:

> Before proud gates attending asses bray,
> Or arrogate with solemn pace the way;
> These grave physicians with their milky cheer,
> The love-sick maid and dwindling beau repair.
> (II, 13-16)

This is a literal description of real four-legged asses, which were driven about from door to door to provide the asses' milk considered a remedy for various fashionable ailments. But the tone of the description suggests that it could apply equally well to two-legged asses, medical doctors with their pose of solemnity, gravity, dignity. It is almost the same technique as that of comparing mud to beauty spots: we smile first at finding asses described like human beings, and then realize the obvious possibilities of inversion—that human beings could equally well be described as asses.

The technique of suddenly reversed perspective demonstrated by these two instances may be considered the central poetic device of *Trivia,* both in its serious and its humorous aspects. Perspective, indeed, is almost the subject of the poem, whose very title insists that the reader be aware of the significance of point of view. Is the word *Trivia* to be taken, as Gay suggests, as the name of the goddess of crossroads? Its Latin origins, of course, support this meaning;[4] but we do not—cannot—take it so, since the word's other, more common, sense wars with its nominal one. Trivia are, by definition, commonplace and insignificant matters. And the duality of the word prepares us for the poem's duality of viewpoint. Truly the affairs of the city, and of each of its citizens, can be seen either as matters of high seriousness or of vast triviality—and Gay never allows us to rest long content with either point of view. The poem shifts its attitudes constantly. This is where its surprises come from, most of its jokes, many of its sharpest insights. Sometimes the double view is inherent in a single word, as when Gay describes the walker who keeps gazing at some girl's face and, as a result, "Shall strike his aking breast against the post" (III, 104). The line's structure suggests that the breast aches *before* striking the post—aches, of course, in a familiar metaphorical sense: with longing for the unattainable woman. But the episode comments on this sort of "aching" by placing it in conjunction with quite another sort: the result of indulgence in fanciful suffering is actual suffering, and the point of view which considers the walker's previous pain important is faintly mocked by his later mishap.

In ways as unimportant as this, or as vital to the poem as the long passage listing signs of the seasons and days (which gradually turns into a joke on the reader, who comes to realize how ludicrous is the assumption that a man of normal awareness needs to examine external signs to know the day of the week), Gay establishes and enforces his double point of view. He recognizes the evil and distraction of the city, but also its charm; he forces the reader to partake of the double recognition.

Throughout *Trivia,* which relies heavily on mythological or pseudo-mythological "decoration" Gay reminds us of his relation to his Latin predecessors—and uses that relation itself as a device to insist on the necessity for shifting attitudes. The longest pseudo-classic sections are two tales, one purporting to relate the origin of bootblacks, the other, the origin of pattens (wooden clogs for elevating shoes above mud or snow). For both phenomena Gay creates elaborate derivations. These narrative interludes are structurally analogous to the long account at the end of the fourth *Georgic* of Aristaeus' quest for information about the blight on his bees. The story involves a complete recapitulation of the Orpheus legend; its function in the *Georgics* is—among other things—to connect the issues involved in beekeeping with the entire course of history and tradition, to emphasize what has already been stressed in other ways: that every concern of mankind is integrally related to every other.

In *Trivia*, with its general tone of faint mockery, the narrative interludes appear to serve no equivalent purpose. Rather, they enforce the ironic commentary which has been offered in other more or less devious ways. The story of the pattens, for example, turns out ultimately to be about "female virtue." Patty, the archetypal "good" country maiden, attracts the attention of Vulcan, who plots how she may be won. First, in the guise of a country blacksmith, he flatters her; then he surrounds her shoes with headless nails, "To save her steps from rains and piercing dews" (I, 264); finally, seeing her suffering from bad weather, he invents the patten to save her health. The conclusion tells us that:

> The God obtain'd his suit; tho' flatt'ry fail,
> Presents with female virtue must prevail.
> The patten now supports each frugal dame,
> Which from the blue-ey'd *Patty* takes the name.
> (I, 279-82)

That the patten, which provides "support" for women of incontestable virtue, should have originated as a means for precipitating virtue's downfall is precisely the kind of joke that Gay enjoys. It provides one more commentary on the ambiguities of civilization and its values by its mode of dealing with one of the civilized accounterments of walkers.

The tale of the bootblack is more closely related to that of Aristaeus. Included for the first time in the second edition of *Trivia*, it traces the bootblack's origins to the union of Cloacina, goddess of sewers, with a mortal scavenger. An elaborate introduction insists that Cloacina in her loose conduct was merely imitating Jove. (There is a faint foreshadowing here of the central joke of *The Beggar's Opera.*) The child resulting from the conjunction of goddess and mortal is apparently an orphan, with no means of support. Consequently, his goddess-mother prays the other gods "to take the foundling's part,/To teach his hands some beneficial art" (II, 151-52). The gods then unite in his service:

> Each Power contributes to relieve the poor:
> With the strong bristles of the mighty boar
> *Diana* forms his brush; the God of day
> A tripod gives, amid the crouded way
> To raise the dirty foot, and ease his toil;
> Kind Neptune fills his vase with fetid oil
> Prest from th' enormous whale; The God of fire,
> From whose dominions smoky clouds aspire,
> Among these gen'rous presents joins his part,
> And aids with soot the new japanning art.
> (II, 157-66)

Cloacina bears these gifts to her child, who is, before her coming, in sad condition: "Pensive through idleness, tears flow'd apace,/Which eas'd his loaded heart, and wash'd his face" (II, 175-76). She informs the boy that his prayers are granted, and that he is to "go thrive" (l. 203) as a bootblack; the youth labors and prospers.

On a very simple level this tale can be seen as elaborate support of Gay's doctrine of work. Yet its effect is rather to undercut that doctrine through its reliance on parody and through the poet's apparent willingness to laugh at his own tendencies toward sentimentality (as in the couplet quoted above, where he saves himself from taking the boy's tears too seriously by recognizing their immediate practical function). The mock-heroic attitudes and material have the usual effect of mock-heroics: to imply a meaningful comparison between the values of the present and those of the past. To summon up the traditional associations with Neptune in order to reveal that the sea-god provides "fetid oil," or to connect the great huntress Diana with a boar's-bristle brush, is to suggest how meaningless images of divinity or of greatness have become in modern times.

The whole concept of the goddess Cloacina, herself a parody figure, has much the same effect. In comparison with Aristaeus, who benefited from his goddess-mother's help by gaining new wisdom and understanding, the bootblack is pitiable indeed. He has gained a mode of making a living, which is, in his circumstances, necessary; yet a world in which one's mode of making a living is of such paramount importance is petty and undignified in comparison with that of Orpheus, as Cloacina, decked with turnip tops and eels, appears degraded by comparison with the goddesses of tradition.

In addition to these two "mythological" interludes, *Trivia* contains many similes, some of epic proportions, whose references depend upon classical knowledge. Frequently these seem more or less arbitrary, merely mocking in their function. Thus, in Book I, the uncurled wig which results from a sudden shower is compared first with the snaky tresses of Alecto, then with the beard of Glaucus; and the point of both comparisons is the same: that modern concerns are ludicrous and undignified by comparison with ancient ones. When Gay compares the bubbling yeast blown back from drays onto the coats of the unwary with the backward-flying javelin of the Parthian (II, 289-96), he implicitly recognizes and laughs at the pettiness of his own concerns throughout this poem; many of his references re-emphasize this comically deprecatory attitude. Occasionally they serve a slightly more complicated purpose. At the end of the account of the hazards of street thieves, for example, Gay offers an image of the crowd clustered round a ballad singer:

> But soon as coach or cart drives rattling on,
> The rabble part, in shoals they backward run.
> So *Jove's* loud bolts the mingled war divide,
> And *Greece* and *Troy* retreat on either side.
> (III, 83-86)

The crowd are seen as warriors, and the point is not merely that the warriors of modern times lack the stature of those of old. The vision of the rabble as engaged in "mingled war" is itself important: the idea of the constant, necessary struggle of the poor provides a meaningful foundation for all the poem's observations—again foreshadowing *The Beggar's Opera*.

Yet for the ultimate effect of *Trivia* the mythological references have a positive as well as an ironic function. Just as *The Shepherd's Week* largely supports pastoral values while mocking the pastoral form, so *Trivia* ultimately affirms the value of the activities it has consistently derided through its formal devices. The consciously false importance that has been lent the material through the classical references seems, in the long run, not entirely false after all. Reading the *Georgics* one learns gradually to consider every activity of the farmer as almost transcendently important, because the farmer's functioning is a microcosm of all human activity: every human endeavor helps meaningfully to define man's place in the cosmos. *Trivia* does not concern itself with the cosmos; it deals only with the limited world of eighteenth-century urban civilization, constantly judged against the grander world of the classical past and the simpler world of the country. Yet the activities of the walker are, finally, significant emblems of the possible range of human effort, and one comes to feel that everything about civilized life can be learned by detailed consideration of walking the streets of London. The poem's language, particularly in the third book, consistently reinforces this idea. When Gay writes:

> ne'er to those dark paths by night retire;
> Mind only safety and contemn the mire,
> Then no impervious courts thy haste detain,
> (III, 129-31)

it is easy to read the lines as allegory, to feel that man's journey through life, a metaphor for writers from Chaucer to Bunyan to Faulkner, is here the controlling figure. Impervious courts as blind alleys, or the impervious courts of kings: the injunction applies equally well to both.

Or, again:

> Ever be watchful to maintain the wall;
> For should'st thou quit thy ground, the rushing throng
> Will with impetuous fury drive along;
> All press to gain those honours thou has lost,
> And rudely shove thee far without the post.
> (III, 206-10)

The rushing throng is a threat to the walker, but equally a threat to the ambitious man; ground lost is lost in either case; the honors one sacrifices are difficult to regain.

To be sure, there are ways out of such dilemmas:

> Though fortune yield thee captive, ne'er despair,
> But seek the constable's consid'rate ear;
> He will reverse the watchman's harsh decree,
> Moved by the rhet'rick of a silver fee.
> Thus would you gain some fav'rite courtier's word;
> Fee not the petty clarks, but bribe my Lord.
> (III, 315-20)

Here the connection between the world of the walker and that of the seeker after fortune is explicit; usually it is not. Yet the connection is there, explicit or not; the more in the third book because it is most concerned with the dangers the walker must face, dangers almost always analogous to those encountered by the wayfarer through life.

III

Gay's duality of viewpoint, then, informs the structure as well as the devices of his poem; and his choice of models for *Trivia*, the very fact that the poem is permeated with references to the classics, helps to make possible the expression of that duality.[5] But the relation of *Trivia* to the *Georgics* exposes the weaknesses as well as the strengths of Gay's work. The poet's sense of ambiguity about proper values might produce confusion rather than complexity, and the *Georgics*, of all models, encouraged the expression of confusion. Georgic imitation was a popular mode of the late seventeenth century and the eighteenth—and a mode frequently employed by writers who did not know quite what they wanted to say.[6] It is significant that Gay chose to write mock-georgic rather than mock-epic. *The Rape of the Lock*, a brilliant example of the latter mode, also conveys duality of attitude (toward its heroine, Belinda, for example, and what she stands for), but does so in a highly disciplined context. In contrast, *Trivia* provides as framework only a loose general organization. With little narrative interest, it must engage the reader through its constantly changing subject matter or through its play of attitudes. Yet the shifting point of view, keeping us always slightly off balance, evokes a sense of complexity which is partly illusory. Gay's ultimate lack of subtlety, at this stage in his poetic career, is exposed particularly in some passages of direct moralizing in which parody and mockery completely disappear, the tension between the values of the present and those of the classical past is no longer an element, the city-country conflict is irrelevant.

James Sutherland, in a brilliant essay on Gay, observes that the poet typically takes his art seriously and wears his morality lightly, that he is by no means "an earnest moralist." [7] Certainly Gay's greatest moral effectiveness comes from concentration on art rather than morality; his straightforward statements of moral sentiment are often sadly lacking in artistic control.

The weakness of poetic effect in such passages derives often from a quite uncharacteristic reliance on abstractions. To abstract brilliantly was one of the great strengths of the best eighteenth-century poets, but it is not among Gay's major poetic talents. The most successful effects in *Trivia* depend on his capacity to render sharp observation real and meaningful. When he attempts the opposite mode in a context of brilliantly revealed concrete realities, the result is disheartening. Thus, speaking of the Christmas season, he moves from his listing of the signs of various times of year to an invocation to charity:

> Now, heav'n-born Charity, thy blessings shed;
> Bid meagre Want uprear her sickly head:
> Bid shiv'ring limbs be warm; let plenty's bowle
> In humble roofs make glad the needy soul.
> See, see, the heav'n-born maid her blessings shed;
> Lo! meagre Want uprears her sickly head;
> Cloath'd are the naked, and the needy glad,
> While selfish Avarice alone is sad.
>
> (II, 443-50)

Gay does not often employ personifications; his turning to them in this instance is emblematic of his attempt to move from his personal mode to a simpler and more conventional procedure. The use of personification in this passage when compared to, say, Collins' mode of dealing with such abstractions, is simple in the extreme. Perhaps the best indication of this fact is the last line, "While selfish Avarice alone is sad." To introduce the character of Avarice here is simply an emphatic way of emblemizing the avaricious man. But the line is singularly unconvincing. No reason has been suggested why *Avarice* should be sad: the avaricious man has not himself been forced to be charitable, and it is hard to imagine that the miser is inevitably saddened by the generosity of others; the train of thought necessary to justify this idea is too complex to be so easily evoked. The adjective-noun combinations are revealingly automatic: *shiv'ring limbs, humble roofs, needy soul.* And they are monotonous, partly because of their predictability, partly because the rhythmical patterns of the pairings tend, in this passage, to be duplicated again and again. The virtual repetition of the lines about heaven-born Charity and meager Want, though clearly intended to achieve balance, underlines the sense of monotony; and this fact seems particularly significant, since elsewhere Gay demonstrates himself to be a master of meaningful repetition. In Book III, for example, he mentions the danger of overturning "the scolding huckster's stall" (1. 124). The adjective seems at first general and conventional, suggesting the huckster's loudness and garrulity, the way in which he harangues pedestrians to buy. The next line repeats the adjective in a new context, and thus freshens it:

> The scolding huckster shall not o'er thee moan,
> But pence exact for nuts and pears o'erthrown.
> (11. 125-26)

Now the passerby suddenly has an individual relationship with the huckster, and the characteristic previously noticed in a generalized and almost patronizing tone becomes specific, personal, and a source for the walker's discomfort.

It is exactly this sort of alertness on the poet's part, this characteristic awareness of shifts and of possibilities, that we miss in the lines on Charity and Want. Alertness is replaced in this passage by reliance on "magic." Instead of making us feel observation converted into insight and shared emotion, Gay depends on simple assertion. He invokes Charity, and Charity promptly does what he wishes; the "problem" is solved as soon as stated, so automatically that we doubt the initial existence of any real difficulty. The sufferings of meager Want, though the poet may multiply images of sickly heads, shivering limbs, needy souls, are not imagined; they are merely poetic counters. The result is the disappointing poetry that Gay often produces, when he attempts direct moral statement. When he describes the evils of beating horses ("O barb'rous men, your cruel breasts assuage,/Why vent ye on the gen'rous steed your rage?" [II, 233-34]); or adjures maidens not to attempt "the dang'rous flame of love" (II, 342), or tells his reader to "Contemplate, mortal, on thy fleeting years" (III, 225), he falls into flatness or confusion or both. Widows and orphans are his conventional emblems of the destructive effects of wealth ("Proud coaches pass regardless of the moan/Of infant orphans, and the widow's groan" [II, 451-52]), and many of his other references seem equally automatic.

At least one interesting passage combines Gay's effective with his ineffective modes of moralizing, and helps to clarify the nature of both:

> See yon bright chariot on its braces swing,
> With *Flanders* mares, and on an arched spring;
> That wretch, to gain an equipage and place,
> Betray'd his sister to a lewd embrace.
> This coach that with the blazon'd 'scutcheon glows,
> Vain of his unknown race, the coxcomb shows.
> Here the brib'd lawyer, sunk in velvet, sleeps;
> The starving orphan, as he passes, weeps;
> There flames a fool, begirt with tinsell'd slaves,
> Who wastes the wealth of a whole race of knaves. . . .
> May the proud chariot never be my fate,
> If purchas'd at so mean, so dear a rate.
> (II, 573-82; 587-88)

This, like so many other passages in *Trivia,* invites one to look at a scene, but the scene is altogether contrived. We are asked to believe that riders in coaches are necessarily corrupt, that the world is inhabited solely by exploiters (wretches, coxcombs, bribed lawyers, fools) and their helpless victims (betrayed sisters, starving orphans). The images depend both upon Gay's usual brilliant observation and upon his powers of abstraction; the observation is generally convincing, while the abstraction seems weak by comparison. Thus the opening evocation of the ease and glamor of the "bright chariot" helps us to accept the condensed story implied by the succeeding couplet: one sees in emblematic terms precisely what the "equipage" is that drives a man to sacrifice his sister; Gay dwells on it with ironically elaborate detail.

A lurid glow envelops the scene: the brightness of the chariot, the glow of the "blazon'd 'scutcheon" on the coach, the flaming light of the fool. The lawyer lolls, "sunk in velvet": velvet is the element which destroys him, he sinks into it like a drowning man. The fool gains his support from merely "tinsell'd slaves": followers bedecked with false wealth. His squandering of wealth is not the aftermath of generations of saving; it is made possible, in this world perceived as totally corrupt, rather by generations of knavery. The final pun on "mean" is well earned: Gay has demonstrated the nature of meanness in a society where wealth is accompanied by degradation. Inasmuch as the scene is visually perceived, it is convincing, and even passionate.

On the other hand, the starving orphan is no more effective here than she is in the simpler couplet quoted earlier. Conveniently appearing as the lawyer passes, she weeps to see him: it is the arrangement of a Sunday school tract. And although the opening description does much to justify the ensuing portrait of the sister-betraying wretch, the portrait clearly *needs* justifying: it derives from rather too simple a moral vision. Gay seems here, as in the passage on charity and in several others, to lapse into sentimentality as he approaches generalization—and the starving orphan is surely as much a generalized abstraction as the figure of Avarice. The sentimentality of the implicit assumption that all virtue resides in poverty, all evil in wealth, does not derive from Virgil, although Virgil, like Gay, prefers rural uprightness to urban sophistication. When, in the *Georgics,* the Latin poet contrasts the corruption of other professions with the peace of rural simplicity, he does so with a much more complex sense of what other professions really involve:

> Some to the Seas, and some to Camps resort,
> And some with Impudence invade the Court.
> In foreign Countries others seek Renown,
> With Wars and Taxes others waste their own.
> And Houses burn, and houshold Gods debase,
> To drink in Bowls which glitt'ring Gems enchase. . . .
> This Wretch in Earth intombs his Golden Ore,
> Hov'ring and brooding on his bury'd Store.
> Some Patriot Fools to pop'lar Praise aspire,
> Or Publick Speeches, which worse Fools admire.[8]

The key words of the passage are those implying moral condemnation: *Impudence, Wretch, Fools.* But the condemnation does not derive from the automatic assumption that certain roles imply corruption: not all patriots, certainly, are patriot fools. Virgil condemns activities—*invading* the court, *wasting* the country, *burning, defacing, entombing, hovering, brooding.* He perceives that activity implies values, that the particular activities he condemns derive from false aspiration (for renown, unused wealth, popular praise); he loathes false aspiration, not any particular profession. He argues his point; Gay merely *asserts* connections which he has not earned the right to. He resembles, in this respect, Bertolt Brecht, whose most famous play, *The Threepenny Opera,* is based on *The Beggar's Opera.* Brecht, like Gay, was a master of observation and sharp definition; he was like Gay, too, in his sympathy for the downtrodden, although the pastoral life was not one of his central preoccupations. But he suffered from the same philosophical weakness: the tendency to equate the underdog automatically with all virtue, the capitalist with all vice. When Brecht *demonstrates* this point (in *Mother Courage,* for example) as he was brilliantly capable of doing, he is likely to win full assent, even from audiences ideologically unsympathetic with him; when he merely asserts it (as in parts of *The Good Woman of Setzuan*) the sentimentality is too blatant. So with Gay—and with Gay, too, our realization that he was capable of more meaningful statement heightens our annoyance at his easy sentimentalities.

It may seem unreasonable to spend so much time belaboring our poet for passages which, after all, occupy a rather small proportion of *Trivia.* Yet sentimentality of the same sort is a key issue in virtually all of Gay's work. The resolution of *Rural Sports* demonstrates the same problem; the weaknesses in *Polly* have a similar source. This fact is not merely psychologically interesting, although obviously psychological speculation of a rather simple sort could be applied to a man who, notoriously concerned himself with acquiring at least a modicum of wealth and position, lashed out so consistently against those who had actually won it. But it is also a fact of central literary significance in understanding Gay's work. Gay's talent was not gigantic, like Swift's or Pope's, and his interests were not fully in tune with those of his age: Professor Sutherland points out, for example, that he probably wrote satire, not his natural form of expression, merely because the literary standards of his time valued satire so highly.[9] Yet one of the most interesting aspects of Gay's work, considered as a whole, is that the poet's lack of complete accord with the values which surrounded him becomes in his work a primary source of poetic strength.

This is not because, like Wordsworth, he had the capacity to strike out against the enveloping conventions to create new conventions of his own. He had no such capacity and made no such effort. But the fact that country fairs and city fruit stalls were not in themselves respectable subjects for poetry forced Gay to find appropriate postures from which to deal with them; if he felt sentimental about the country he found it necessary on the whole to conceal this fact with elaborate layers of parody and irony. These layers give his work its greatest poetic force; these efforts to conceal, to make respectable, provide the complexity, the richness, that we often admire. His instinct was sound in choosing classical models, and in selecting the particular models he employs—for the models, too, and his feelings about them, offer a method of "distancing," of cultivating an attitude toward his material rather than simply indulging his automatic, and frequently uninteresting, responses.

But the "bad," straightforward, sentimental passages suggest that by the severest tests *Trivia* is not ultimately completely successful. Its very real wit does not operate in the service of a sufficiently complex moral vision. The values which emerge from the poem are solid enough, but discomfitingly simple; hard work and honesty are good, corruption and venereal disease are bad. Such values can be easily held, but they do not provide an adequate foundation for serious social criticism. We miss Pope's examination of the *nature* of corruption, miss the passion of the poet whose ideas have been struggled for. In its poetic devices, in its complex relation to Virgil, in the awareness it demonstrates of the moral implications of observation, *Trivia* seems potentially a more weighty poem than it quite manages to be.

CHAPTER 3

"Life Is a Jest"

TO be fashionable in 1720 a poet wrote satire. The age was so corrupt, in the opinion of its dominant literary figures, that the satirist's passion supplied the only adequate mode of commenting on it. For Swift and Pope, such passion was the inevitable reaction to the prevalence of vulgarity, greed, and stupidity; for their lesser contemporaries, the imitation of passion provided at least a technique for poetic glibness.

Gay, in 1720, was ready to publish his first collection of poems: a quarto edition in two volumes, sold by subscription. Primarily a money-making venture (he actually earned a thousand pounds or more from it),[1] it was also, of course, an artistic one, necessitating evaluation and selectivity on Gay's part: he did not publish all the poems he had printed before.[2] The poems included, however, demonstrate a wide range—and a marked tendency toward satire. *Trivia* had more nearly approached satiric vigor than had *The Shepherd's Week;* some of the verse epistles in the 1720 volume show an even firmer (although still wavering) commitment to the ideal of satiric intensity.

One of the less serious epistles, "To A Young Lady with Some Lampreys" (printed for the first time in this collection), is representative of both the subtlety and the limitations which Gay demonstrates in these pieces. The joke of the poem, and its theme, is that seafood in general and lampreys in particular are thought to be aphrodisiac, and hence an improper present from a man to a girl of fifteen. The opening sequence, one of the best in the poem, establishes a general context:

With lovers 'twas of old the fashion
By presents to convey their passion;
No matter what the gift they sent,

> The Lady saw that love was meant.
> Fair *Atalanta,* as a favour,
> Took the boar's head her Hero gave her;
> Nor could the bristly thing affront her,
> 'Twas a fit present from a hunter.
> When Squires send woodcocks to the dame,
> It serves to show their absent flame. . . .
> How many mercenary matches
> Have sprung from Di'mond-rings and watches!
> (11. 1-10, 13-14)

The poem pretends to be no more than an occasional piece, yet this setting of the stage suggests a wider purpose. The gift of lampreys is to be considered in the context of the mythical past of Atalanta and of the satirically perceived present of mercenary matches. That we are to take neither context altogether seriously is suggested by the pervasive lightness of the feminine rhymes, the colloquial tone of the contractions, and the poet's failure to dwell on any single point. On the other hand, beneath the surface of polite frivolity lurks observation so sharp and precise that it implies firm value judgments. The lines on Atalanta, for example, seem merely to illustrate that in ancient times, as in modern, women accept gifts of any sort as indications of passion. Yet Atalanta's acceptance of the gift turns out to be full of scorn, only nominally courteous. The boar's head achieved by the hero is to her a "bristly thing"; the phrase captures perfectly the tone of sophisticated but empty feminine gentility. " 'Twas a fit present from a hunter" emphasizes Atalanta's scorn by its implication that nothing more could be expected from a mere hunter and by its hinted feminine superiority to the pursuits which men take with such ludicrous seriousness. But the ambiguities cut also in the opposite direction in the next couplet, which suggests that perhaps men take women no more seriously than women do men: the "absent flame" of the squire may indicate merely that the squire is absent and sends woodcocks as testimony of his love even when he is away hunting; but it may also suggest that the flame is absent when the lover is absent, that hunting replaces love as an interest (the lover sends woodcocks which testify his skill but mean little to his lady), that this squire resembles Pope's, who "loves you best of all things—but his horse." The mercenary matches of the present seem, in this context, in no way essentially different from the romances of the past: true acceptance between men and women is equally absent from both.

Once this cynical point of view is suggested, Gay pleads his own case, with disarming casualness, employing the same bantering tone to convey his own ambiguities of attitude. A poet, he informs us, should not send expensive presents which would drain his pocket; he should rather "send songs that cost him nought,/Nor even be prodigal of thought" (ll. 17-18). Why, then, does Gay himself offer lampreys? Posing the question, he supplies no immediate answer to it; instead, he begins to speculate elaborately about the feminine reactions to his gift. He imagines in detail the comments of the aunt, who thinks the poet, on the basis of his gift, a "filthy fellow" (l. 33), who explains that shepherdesses are only chaste because they live on salad and that Diana's maids, if they ate lampreys, would all lie around "like Calisto" (l. 46). Her moral summary provides the poem's best stanza:

> Who has her virtue in her power?
> Each day has its unguarded hour;
> Always in danger of undoing,
> A prawn, a shrimp may prove our ruin!
> (ll. 37-40)

The effect of the lines depends upon their perfect accuracy of tone, the precision with which they convey the note of conventional moral admonition and undercut it by the ludicrous triviality of content. The aunt's worrying over the dangers of a prawn or shrimp is emblematic of her entire moral condition, her total absorption in trivia.

After the lack of real feminine values is thus benignly exposed, Gay is in a position finally to answer the question posed earlier: why lampreys? The answer is simple: the recipient of his gift has an aphrodisiac effect on the poet; consequently lampreys are the appropriate tribute. But the effect of this confession is quite different from what it would have been earlier in the poem; it has been modified by the elaborate image of feminine hypocrisy against which the poet's comparatively brutal honesty must be judged. "Your eyes, lips, breasts," he says, "are so provoking" that you "set my heart more cock-a-hoop,/Than could whole seas of craw-fish soup" (11. 52-54). "Provoking" is the key word: it implies the ultimate judgment of all feminine prudery, which coexists with feminine provocativeness, as deliberate attempts to lure men. The poet's frank lust is merely the equivalent of the women's concealed lechery; lust may be shocking, but its honesty makes it morally preferable to the concealment practiced by the opposite sex.

Yet this reading is misleading, for it suggests far more satiric bite and moral weight than the poem actually has. The epistle's casualness of tone subtracts importantly from the moral seriousness of the piece as a whole. A comic poem, this has no spirit of reform. Pope observed that comedy always implies censure, but for Gay no such correlation seems to exist: however precisely he may define human—and here particularly feminine—weakness, he always *accepts* that weakness. The note of acceptance, amused but unbitter, is Gay's special note; it dominates his famous epitaph for himself:

> Life is a jest; and all things show it.
> I thought so once; but now I know it.

The piece on the lampreys, not particularly important in itself, is quite representative of Gay's special quality in the 1720 volume. It relies on no specific model; it manifests Gay's particular sort of irony, which depends upon brilliantly accurate observation; it demonstrates how irony can be absorbed in a pervasive gentleness of tone. Gay knows himself to be a part of the world which he defines; he is in this respect quite unlike Pope, quite unlike any of the great satirists, all of whom are capable of assuming the godlike *persona* which gives their criticism maximum force.

Maynard Mack, in a well-known essay called "The Muse of Satire," points out that satire is necessarily dominated by "a fictional perspective on the real world,"[3] that the satiric speaker in a poem must be "an assumed identity, a *persona*" (p. 227). He identifies three distinct roles which Pope characteristically assumes: that of "*vir bonus,* the plain good private citizen" (228); that of *ingenu,* the naïve, unsophisticated observer; and, most authoritative of all, that of public defender, the hero who passionately supports values.[4]

The terminology with which Professor Mack defines Pope's typical roles illuminates Gay's inadequacies as a satirist. The truth is that Gay apparently finds it inordinately difficult to maintain for long a fictional role and that the voice of the public defender seems impossible for him to achieve. We shall encounter many instances in which he presents himself as *naïf*; the satiric force of this *persona*, however, largely disappears unless the poet also assumes the authority of some more adult role. Gay could manage the part of "plain private citizen"; his limited satiric success depends largely on his evocation of this image. But much of the time he is too manifestly a part of the society he mocks, quite unable to summon any real distance from it. Swift, in his verses "On the Death of Dr. Swift," *plays the role* of a participant in the evils he criticizes; when he gradually substitutes the image of himself as godlike in his elevation above the pettiness of his contemporaries, the new role gains power by its contrast with the old. But for Gay the position of participant is not controlled fiction. The world which he sees with amused clarity is the one he inhabits, which he actually helps to create. He does not separate himself by implication from the characters in his poems: if he is not a hypocrite, like the women he depicts, he is lustful; and both qualities are equally clearly human frailties.

"To a Lady on her Passion for Old China," makes a similar point even more emphatically, with its explicit equation of various kinds of human weakness. It is thematically and tonally more complicated than the epistle about the lampreys. Laura loves old china, the poet loves Laura; both passions are of the same sort. And both may be equated also with the passions of the "Philosophers more grave than wise" who "Hunt science down in butterflies" (11. 19-20), or of the scientist who "digs for knowledge, like a mole" (1. 24) until he has so perfected his knowledge of shells that "No fish that swims knows more than he!" (1. 26). These passions are all equally irrational, and all are alike focused on fragile objects. Everything is as likely as china to "break": the love of china itself breaks the rest of Laura (1. 10); the hopes of ambition swell, shine, and break "like bubbles" (11. 57-58); courtiers' promises are readily broken (1. 60); mistresses break the fortune and the sleep of their possessors (11. 61-62); the man who chooses the country

"Breaks all the comforts of his wife" (1. 64), but if he goes to the town, the wife is likely to "break her vow" (1. 66). Finally the poem is resolved in terms of the same metaphor:

> Love, *Laura*, love, while youth is warm,
> For each new winter breaks a cham;
> And woman's not like *China* sold,
> But cheaper grows in growing old;
> Then quickly chuse the prudent part,
> Or else you break a faithful heart.
> (11. 67-72)

The notion of fragility becomes thus a grounds for asserting the difference rather than the similarity between the passion of love and the passion for china: women are *not* ultimately like china, because they inevitably lose charm rather than gain it as they age. The poet in effect invites the woman to allow herself deliberately to be "flawed": the metaphoric equivalence between the destruction of chastity and the flawing of a china jar which appears in "The Rape of the Lock" ("Whether a nymph should break Diana's law,/Or some rare china jar receive a flaw") is also implicit here. Indeed, it is quite explicit earlier in the poem:

> She who before was highest priz'd,
> Is for a crack or flaw despis'd.
> (11. 39-40)

The final paradox is that the greatest good, in an irrational world, is the willing acceptance of feminine frailty—because the alternative, the breaking of a "faithful" (*i.e.*, enduring, non-fragile) heart would be the most dreadfully destructive breakage possible.

The total attitude toward humanity remains constant. The poet observes and understands human weakness; finds it comic though pathetic, and, because of his own lively sense of pleasurable involvement in the general irrationality, cannot be bitter or fierce. The complex tone implied by this attitude is discernable in most of Gay's epistles, both major and minor. Whether he merely recounts the mundane events of a journey to Exeter ("An Epistle to the Right Honourable the Earl of Burlington") or praises the author of the land-tax bill ("To My Ingenious and Worthy Friend W[illiam] L[owndes], Esq."), his criticism is always qualified by his sense of his own participation in the vices and follies of mankind; and his praise is modified by his awareness of the essential ludicrousness of most human endeavor. He has the sharp perception of the innocent, but his fresh perspective is not supported by any real authority. The modulation from innocence to authoritative indignation which Pope could manage so masterfully was apparently beyond Gay's reach.

To be sure, Gay's satiric bite is sometimes sharper in the longer epistles than it is in either of the shorter ones we have thus far considered. In the "Epistle to the Right Honourable William Pulteney, Esq.," for example, he presents himself as merely the ordinary Englishman, a combination of naïf and "plain good man." He disarms criticism by forestalling it:

> Yes, I can sagely, when the times are past,
> Laugh at those follys which I strove to taste
> (11. 3-4)

But the poem contains moments of real satiric vigor, quite inappropriate to the author's pose of naïveté, but self-justifying by their clarity and force:

> He dresses, fences. What avails to know?
> For women chuse their men, like silks, for show.
> (11. 59-60)

The couplet is Popean in its emphasis and economy; it conveys a convincing scorn for the values of those who reduce men in their considerations to the level of things. The same implicit assumption of the high value of genuine humanity as a standard, never overtly defined but always in the background, dictates both the technique and the content of much in the satiric epistles.

In the "Epistle to Pulteney," stress on man's essential humanity and the various possible alternatives to recognition of this humanity are of central thematic importance. Men might, for example, be perceived (as in Gay's own *Fables*) to be in their degradation essentially animals:

> In *Paris,* there's a race of animals,
> (I've seen them at their Operas and Balls.)
> They stand erect, they dance when-e'er they walk,
> Monkeys in action, perroquets in talk;
> They're crown'd with feathers, like the cockatoo,
> And, like camelions, daily change their hue.
> (11. 31-36)

Gay takes no responsibility for this description: it purports to be not his own insight but the comments that the famous Dampier would offer, "without ill-meaning satire" (1. 29), if he had the task of defining the Parisian nature. The implication is that Gay himself is unwilling to offer such "easy truth" (1. 41), and his disclaimer of responsibility gives added satiric bite to the description which follows, in which men are seen, on the whole, not as animals but as things. The "charm" of men is in their apparel; the wit is wretched and forlorn "Whose gummy hat no scarlet plumes adorn" (1. 48), and even "though Apollo dictate from his tongue" (1. 53) he can expect no approval while he "wants th' assurance of brocade and lace" (1. 54).

If women judge men by their apparel, they are equally willing to treat themselves as objects: Corinna, who frequently loses at cards, finally "pawns her person for the sharper's loan" (1. 88) and is ironically praised by the poet for her integrity in paying debts of honor. Madame "puts on her Opera face" (1. 94) as artificially as she dons her gown, and the brilliance of her cheeks is compared not with that of real flowers but with the "silken rose" on her dress (11. 97-98). The people in the Tuilleries are merely "crowds of rustling manteaus" (1. 134); the fop who steps forth to accost the poet is recognized not by his face but by "the bold embroidery of his vest" (1. 138); his questions about London equate Christianity with "daily soups." At the opera the young men on stage, identified as "embroider'd youth" (1. 187), are admired for their gold-clocked stockings. Gay depicts a society in which clothes, more important than men, provide the ultimate standard of judgment, and in which men—and women—seem essentially no more than their clothes.

In such a context, the poem's discussions of sexual activity acquire special irony. The point is not merely that a lady can sin "for scarves, clock'd stockings, knots and shoes" (1. 172) because her own charms, evaluated by the same standards as clothes, have "grown cheap by constant use" (1. 171); this is simple and obvious enough. The more subtle, and more important, point is that all human activity, even so basic an affirmation of life as sexual encounters, becomes, given the pervading system of values, essentially mechanical. The most vivid single image of mechanization is of audience and actors at the opera reacting like clockwork when the orchestra begins:

> But hark! the full *Orchestra* strike the strings;
> The Hero strutts, and the whole audience sings.
> (11. 191-92)

But the extensive sex lives of all the characters in this panorama are almost equally mechanized. Some women regulate their promiscuity by formal principles: "She scorns th' ignoble love of feeble pages,/But with three Abbots in one night engages" (11. 175-76); by a similar arbitrary rule, love flies the town for the woods in the springtime. With really brilliant economy, Gay conveys the entire scheme of things in a couplet:

> Then *Chelsea's* meads o'erhear perfidious vows,
> And the prest grass defrauds the grazing cows.
> (11. 105-06)

The treachery of the vows is as established a part of the procedure as the lovers' pressing down of the grass—which is treachery to the natural order. Everything in this world is arbitrary convention: "Stretch'd on the grass the shepherd sighs his pain,/And on the grass what shepherd sighs in vain?" (11. 115-16). The choice of grass as a milieu for lovemaking means no more than the choice of velvet couches; the two are finally explicitly equated, with the implied comment that grass may be preferable because couches are expensive:

> But since at Court the rural taste is lost,
> What mighty summs have velvet couches cost!
> (11. 131-32)

There are moments of real disgust in Gay's account of this highly structured, artificial system of life, but the predominant tone is gentle amusement at the follies of mankind. Finally, the poem provides an account of its positive standards, what Professor Mack calls the "antithesis layer"; here Gay's satiric weakness is sharply revealed. England and her ruler now exemplify the good king and the good country, although in England, too, "fools of various character abound" (1. 258) (the epistle's earlier satire of women, of course, is directed at Englishwomen as much as at their French counterparts). The greatness of England is its solid support of commercial activity:

> Happy, thrice happy shall the monarch reign,
> Where guardian laws despotic power restrain!
> There shall the ploughshare break the stubborn land,
> And bending harvests tire the peasant's hand:
> There liberty her settled mansion boasts,
> There commerce plenty brings from foreign coasts.
> (11. 247-52)

This is in some general sense relevant to the discussion it follows: it opposes to the mechanized chaos of France an eighteenth-century vision of "natural" hierarchical order in England. Yet it is unconvincing, inadequate, and confusing. Pope concludes his "Epistle to Burlington" with a not entirely dissimilar vision of national glory; his exalted tone exemplifies what Gay vainly tried to achieve. But Pope's exaltation is *earned,* as Gay's is not. The positive images which Pope finally offers reflect and comment on the negative ones that have preceded them; the energy with which he has denounced the misuse of riches justifies the intensity with which he praises the proper employment of wealth. It is quite otherwise with Gay. The relation of man to nature has been hardly at all a theme of his poem; that of kings to subjects is even more remote from his main concerns. And the final glorification of commerce is worse than irrelevant: a poet can hardly afford to praise commercial success as a goal while deriding the activities of a society based on materialistic standards. Gay does not seem to perceive the relation between commerce and materialism. He partly accepts the standards he condemns; as a result, he cannot approach the authoritative passion of the true satirist.

Preoccupation with money is central in several of these epistles and the ambiguities of Gay's attitudes toward money help to define the ambiguities of his stance as a satirist. He lacks—or seems in these comparatively early poems to lack—the satirist's special sophistication. The uncomfortable naïveté of *A Letter to a Lady, Occasioned by the Arrival of Her Royal Highness,* which Sven Armens describes accurately enough as "a burlesque on how to write a eulogistic poem,"[5] persists in poems lacking the excuse of burlesque:

> Since all my schemes were baulk'd, my last resort,
> I left the Muses to frequent the Court. . . .
> Places, I found, were daily giv'n away,
> And yet no friendly Gazette mention'd Gay.
> I ask'd a friend what method to pursue;
> He cried, I want a place as well as you.
> (11. 95-96, 101-04)

The "innocence" of the poet's clear assumption that he deserves rewards like any other man and his "disillusionment" when he stumbles over the universality of such hopes are not displeasing. But when Gay goes on in his own voice (11. 107-12) to explain that he cannot write successfully without the place at court that would make writing easy, we may be reminded of the familiar argument of the student who claims that he cannot write good themes because he is discouraged by not getting good grades. There is a grain of truth in his logic, as in Gay's, but the accompanying revelation of self-pity and self-regard is hardly calculated to produce the respect which the successful satirist must earn from his readers.

To be sure, the *Letter to a Lady* does not purport to be a satiric poem. But the attitudes revealed in it persist in some of the avowedly satiric epistles. Patronage is the subject of the "Epistle to the Right Honourable Paul Methuen, Esq.," in which Gay makes some apparent effort to preserve the proper satiric distance between himself and his subject matter. The poem has moments of brilliance, as when Gay, listing the ways for an author "to be great" (1. 17), advises:

> Or if you chuse more sure and ready ways,
> Spatter a Minister with fulsome praise:
> Launch out with freedom, flatter him enough;
> Fear not, all men are dedication-proof.
> (11. 19-22)

Here the poet demonstrates once more his capacity to perceive and fully realize the literal force of metaphors. Or he is capable of epigrammatic condensation: "Against th'ungrateful age these authors roar,/And fancy learning starves because they're poor" (11. 35-36). But the impact of this couplet is considerably weakened when, a few lines later, Gay comments on his own situation:

> Yet let not me of grievances complain,
> Who (though the meanest of the Muse's train)
> Can boast subscriptions to my humble lays,
> And mingle profit with my little praise.
> (11. 41-44)

Both the tone (the mechanical disclaimers, the smug self-satisfaction) and the implied value system are disturbing: the suggestion is clear that money is, in effect, the ultimate criterion of artistic as well as commercial value.

The particular kind of innocence which this passage manifests—the naïve pleasure at having, in some clearly demonstrable sense, "succeeded"—may be appealing in the man, but it is no valid part of the satirist's equipment. It is manifested in other ways in this poem (not simply in attitudes toward money), and in each case it is equally destructive to Gay's pretensions as satirist. When, for example, he praises Burlington's taste, he remarks,

> While *Burlington's* proportion'd columns rise,
> Does not he stand the gaze of envious eyes?
> Doors, windows, are condemn'd by passing fools,
> Who know not that they damn *Palladio's* rules.
> (11. 65-68)

The last line reveals the poet's self-satisfaction at being "in the know" himself. Knowing better than to expose his own ignorance in such a fashion, he mocks those who do not share his sophistication—but surely it is significant that he mocks them not for lack of taste but, snobbishly, for lack of knowledge. Again, slightly earlier in the poem (11. 51-60), he praises the contemporary artist William Kent, comparing him explicitly to Raphael. He may perhaps be excused for disproportionate adulation of one who was later to illustrate his *Fables*, but he thus compromises his own stated values. In the "Epistle to Pulteney" he had derided Frenchmen who equate Rigaud (a minor French painter) with Raphael on grounds essentially of nationality; Gay is guilty here of similar weakness—and it is not a weakness a satirist can afford. Perfect clarity of standards we always demand of the satirist; it is the only conceivable foundation for his art. And such clarity Gay achieves only sporadically. The childlike quality of his personality, the curious and persistent innocence that made his friends love him and vie with one another in efforts to take care of him—these qualities made the man lovable, but frequently weakened the poet.

That Gay was in some sense conscious of the ambiguities of his attitude toward money is suggested by the fact that in two of his verse epistles he dealt explicitly with the relation between the man of commerce and the poet. A genuine *jeu d'esprit*, with comic force if little satiric bite, is the epistle "To My Ingenious and Worthy Friend, W[illiam] L[owndes], Esq., Author of that Celebrated Treatise in Folio Called the "Land-Tax Bill." Its central joke is to treat a parliamentary bill as though it were a work of literature. Poets, Gay points out at the outset, who write with no desire for money win fame for their artistic creation. The man who composes a bill which raises millions of pounds a year really deserves fame as well: "Great L[owndes] his praise should swell the trump of fame,/And *Rapes* and *Wapentakes* resound his name" (11. 11-12). (Rapes and wapentakes are English administrative divisions, subdivisions of counties.) Homer was known for singing the chiefs and heroes of Greece; Lowndes deserves more for listing "five thousand Knights and Squires,/Their seats, their citys, parishes, and shires" (11. 16-17). Yet it is clear enough that Lowndes is neither poet nor historian. How then to define his genius? Gay offers the telling answer: "Satyr is thy talent; and each lash/Makes the rich Miser tremble o'er his cash" (11. 30-31). This is the high spot of the poem, which trails off at the end after some detailed explanations of Lowndes' superiority to other sorts of men of letters in permanence and power.

Sven Armens asserts that this epistle demonstrates Gay's true satiric talent. "Gay feels," he writes, "that the poet should have some guarantee of economic security in a society that values knowledge. And the fact that he does not have such security is indirect proof that his society does not value knowledge. The distortion of the use of words, instruments of inspiration and knowledge, to make money . . . , while the real use of words for the rational communication of values is neglected, constitutes the basic perversion of society satirized in this epistle." And again, in summary, "This epistle is then a fine example of Gay's satiric railery and his use of irony to expose false social values." [6]

But surely this epistle is less satiric and more complicated than Sven Armens perceives. No one can blame the poet for wanting, like other men, "some guarantee of economic security." Yet the fact that he persistently records this desire in his poems dealing with money modifies any conceivable satiric effect. Gay describes a perverted world in which only the man who affects people economically can conceivably exercise the sort of power traditionally reserved to the satirist; but in some significant way the poet, by his own concern with money, participates in its perversions. The railery which Sven Armens perceives is present, but the fact that it must be partly self-railery modifies the tone and leaves the reader not with the sense that false values have been ruthlessly exposed—as Pope would expose them—but that Gay has seen and recorded a joke on himself and his society. He believes satire to be a "lash," but his own early poetry rarely stings, never lacerates.

The full complexity and ambiguity of his attitude emerges in the *Panegyrical Epistle to Mr. Thomas Snow,* which was published separately in 1721. Thomas Snow, a goldsmith who made a fortune buying and selling shares of the South Sea Company, was thus indirectly one of the causes of Gay's losing money in the "South Sea Bubble," a dark episode in England's economic history. In January, 1720, Parliament accepted a proposal from the South Sea Company to take over the national debt (£51,000,000) on favorable terms. The company, which monopolized English trade in the West Indies, expected a resultant rise in the price of its shares, a rise which indeed took place. The public clamored to buy, wild speculation ensued, and the price of the shares rose 1,000 percent in August before the bottom dropped out of the market in September.[7] Gay had been given some stock in the South Sea Company by a friend, and he invested virtually his entire small fortune in the venture.[8] Most of it, of course, was lost, and the "Epistle to Snow" comments on the disaster.

It is a powerful, if not altogether lucid, poem; its subject, more explicitly than ever, is the relation between the poet and the man of business. Snow, whose very name serves an ironic function, is perceived as an essentially demonic figure, although he is subtly and ironically compared, as Sven Armens perceptively observes, with Ulysses and Achilles.[9] Yet his demonic aspect is less important, ultimately, than his "realism"—or perhaps it is more accurate to say that his sinister qualities are the direct result of his realism.

Snow is realistic in occupying himself almost entirely with real objects. The South Sea Company dealt in imaginary profits; Snow's are genuine. The search for wealth in Peru yielded few results; Snow's shop, on the other hand, "unexhausted," is a richer Peru. The gold that "blackens" Snow's hand is genuine; he has nothing to do, like such lesser moneylenders, as "Vulture" Hopkins, with merely "ideal debts." To him is opposed the typical poet, "Who live[s] on fancy, and can feed on air" (l. 20), "Who ne'er enjoy'd a guinea but in dreams" (l. 22), who contemplates "millions of imaginary gold" (l. 24). In a world of reality the poet is the image of the eternal victim, a man of "fancies wild" (l. 25); Snow is one "whose judgment scorns poetic flights" (l. 28). And in this difference lies the central meaning of the epistle.

The ultimate question, in this as in so many other works of literature, is how to define reality. The conflict of values between unworldly poet and realistic businessman is resolved by a little fable about life in an insane asylum—one explicitly defined as the retreat of genuine wisdom from a mad world. (The tale, indeed, inevitably reminds one of Dryden's "Great wits are sure to madness near allied.")

Two of the asylum's inmates are a poet and a banker, counterparts in the insane world of the anonymous poet who appeared earlier and of Snow himself. The banker occupies himself with elaborating and contemplating an imaginary estate, which he offers the poet the dubious privilege of buying for £10,000. When the poet accepts this offer, the banker, in a moment of lucidity, realizes that both the estate and the payment he may get for it are imaginary, but he sees the opportunity for earning at least a genuine penny. "Give me a Penny," he commands, "and thy Contract's void" (1. 65). But the poet, being a poet, no more has a penny than he has £10,000. He reacts with righteous indignation to the banker's suggestion; scorning the notion that he should "compound" his debts, he makes ten notches in the skewer that holds a tattered rug round his neck in lieu of a cloak, and cries defiantly, "There, take my Tally of Ten Thousand Pound" (1. 71).

A tally can by definition be a record either of a debt or of a payment. In this case it records a debt—but the ambiguity is obviously significant, for the official acknowledgment of a debt clearly seems to the poet, in terms of some obscure notion of honor, comparable to the paying of it. The satiric implications of this little fable are extremely complicated. If the fable defines the eternal struggle of realist and romantic, it does little to clarify Gay's attitude toward either. The poet "wins" in the little story—wins because in a world unconnected to actuality the inhabitant with the least awareness of reality must triumph: the poet is well adapted to life in an insane asylum. Although he is clearly the moral superior of the banker, he, too, is mocked. His indignation, his cry of defiance, derive from some obscure notion of honor, equally ridiculous within and outside the context of an asylum. Context alone makes the banker ludicrous: his limited concern with concrete actuality becomes meaningless in a madhouse. But has anything really been said about the value of such standards in another setting? Gay seems this time to have dealt with the problem of the poet's stance by refusing to assume any position at all. His story must stand in its own terms, with all its ambiguities; and however valuable we have discovered ambiguity to be, ambiguity of standards is a dangerous luxury for satirists.

It is easy to explain the confusion of values on the basis of biographical evidence, to say that Gay expresses his self-disgust at having allowed himself to be duped, as well as his anger at the dupers. Yet the ambiguity of emphasis, in the light of the other poems Gay was publishing about the same time, seems to come from a deeper split in values than the specific episode might suggest. The confusion in this poem over whether the poet or the banker is a more fitting object of scorn may be the confusion of a writer who found it difficult to define precisely his own relation to commercial values.

II

Ambiguity of values was actually the subject of many of the poems in the 1720 volume, with the poet's own mixed attitudes working sometimes for, sometimes against maximum poetic effect. The eclogues, all except one published in 1720 for the first time, are especially interesting in relation to this theme of ambiguity. Three of the five are so-called "town eclogues," in which Gay uses essentially the same device as in *Trivia:* a structural scheme traditionally reserved for country matters as a mode of comment on the perversion of urban values. One eclogue, "The Espousal," is a "Quaker eclogue"; only one—and by far the best—deals directly with the country. This is "The Birth of the Squire," and even it, with its constant implicit reference to Virgil's prophetic fourth eclogue, contrasts the traditional pastoral values with their modern degradation.

Gay's emphasis, in the three town eclogues, is specifically on the ambiguities of attitude which life in the city seems almost necessarily to foster. "The Toilette," which had been published in 1716 in a volume entitled *Court Poems,* with a piece by Pope and one by Lady Mary Wortley Montague, describes the mental conflicts of a thirty-five-year-old ex-belle named Lydia. She inhabits a world in which almost everything can be assumed to be false:

> False are the loose Coquet's inveigling airs,
> False is the pompous grief of youthful heirs,
> False is the cringing courtier's plighted word,
> False are the dice when gamesters stamp the board,
> False is the sprightly widow's publick tear;
> Yet these to *Damon's* oaths are all sincere.
>
> (11. 73-78)

In such a world love is the falsest value of all. To be sure, this is only Lydia's opinion, yet nothing in the town eclogues suggests even the possibility of genuine, disinterested, enduring love which would contradict all the assumptions of the society.

Youth and beauty are primary values in the world of the poem and Lydia feels inadequate because of her inability to retain either quality. Lacking them, she can only pretend to them; there is no feasible alternative mode of conduct.

> What shall I do? how spend the hateful day?
> At chappel shall I wear the morn away?
> Who there frequents at these unmodish hours,
> But ancient matrons with their frizled tow'rs,
> And gray religious maids? my presence there
> Amid that sober train wou'd own despair;
> Nor am I yet so old; nor is my glance
> As yet fixt wholy to devotion's trance.
> (11. 43-50)

The only really acceptable "devotion" is "the dumb devotion of her glass" (1. 16) in which Lydia can more wholeheartedly participate.

The passage in which Lydia considers the possibility of spending the morning at chapel is an excellent example of the complex attitude projected by the poem and of its lack of satiric energy. Gay does not simply condemn his subject for her frivolity, even in so extreme an instance as this of her lack of awareness. Instead, the condemnation is strikingly qualified by sympathy—not admiration, such as Pope, for example feels for his Belinda in "The Rape of the Lock," but awareness of the poignancy and difficulty of the woman's dilemma. There are, to be sure, frequent direct stabs at Lydia:

> She smooths her brow, and frizles forth her hairs,
> And fancys youthful dress gives youthful airs;
> With crimson wooll she fixes ev'ry grace,
> That not a blush can discompose her face.
> (11. 17-20)

But the eclogue's dominant tone is more accurately represented by the passage on chapel, in which the implicit criticism of Lydia for failing to recognize the reality of religious experience is partly counteracted by the implicit insistence that such recognition would be impossible in this society. Lydia may truly wish for alternative ways of spending her time; there are simply none open to her. She decides, after rejecting chapel, to spend her morning wandering through shops; then she gives up that idea because "then remembrance will my grief renew,/'Twas there the raffling dice false *Damon* threw" (11. 57-58). Her grief appears genuine enough, although she perceives quite accurately the evils of conventional married life:

> *Damon* is practis'd in the modish life,
> Can hate, and yet be civil to a wife.
> He games; he swears; he drinks; he fights; he roves;
> Yet *Chloe* can believe he fondly loves.
> Mistress and wife can well supply his need,
> A miss for pleasure, and a wife for breed.
> (11. 81-86)

This description is sour grapes: Lydia is trying to convince herself that her former lover, now possessed by Chloe, is not worth having after all. But it is also perfectly accurate in its evocation of the sort of marriage depicted in, for example, *The Way of the World;* in its energy and economy it is one of the best passages in the poem. It, too, emphasizes the impossibility of alternatives: no meaningful choice is available to Lydia. If she is capable of genuine feeling, there is no appropriate, nonludicrous mode for expressing it. At the end of the poem, the maid's flattery resolves her struggle: "Strait *Lydia* smil'd; the comb adjusts her locks,/And at the Play-house *Harry* keeps her box" (11. 105-06). Lydia is, like everyone else, ultimately superficial, easily distracted from her grief and quite willing to move on to a new lover if one is available. But the context of the poem has already convinced the reader that superficiality represents the only conceivable principle of conduct in this society.

Swift claimed to hate and detest the animal man but to love John, Peter, Thomas; it is by no means uncommon for the satirist to make sharp distinctions between his attitude toward a society and his feelings about specific members of that society. But Gay's split in attitude toward the group and toward individuals in it weakens his satire; it gives the town eclogues, too, his characteristic note of gentleness. If Pope or Swift feels sympathy or respect for individuals, such sympathy or respect is used, in a satiric context, for strongly focused contrast: the image of the Man of Ross, in Pope's third Moral Epistle, comments on the many negative images that precede and follow it. In "The Toilette" there are *no* entirely negative images. Lydia is criticized for painting her face, for trying superficially to restore the appearance of her vanished youth, but this criticism is counteracted by a context which insists that she can hardly do otherwise. Damon is condemned, in the passage quoted above, as the type of the modish husband, but he can be thus condemned only because he is here perceived as a type rather than an individual. The grounds of Gay's sympathy with Lydia is no special excellence which he sees in her; it is simply his recognition of her essential existence *as a person.* Once he becomes conscious that the would-be victims of his satire are individual human beings, as well as representatives of a corrupt society, his bite is lost; the satirist's energy disappears in the compassion of one fully conscious of his own participation in human frailty and of the fact that, given life is a jest and all things show it, there is no particular reason to condemn fiercely any specific examples of the universal weakness—or even viciousness—of mankind.

In the other town eclogues, the themes announced in "The Toilette" are elaborated. "The Tea-Table" is a dialogue between two belles in which the cattishness demonstrated by Lydia in her discussion of Chloe is more fully demonstrated. The lack of satiric force comes in this poem from a different cause. In "The Toilette" the real subject of the poem is the mental activity of a woman divided between adherence to superficial social standards and a weak but real desire to find alternatives to these standards. The poet's attitude toward his subject is as ambiguous as her own state of mind: he, too, is divided between sympathy for Lydia as a human being and condemnation of her as a type. In the discussion between Doris and Melanthe in the second town eclogue, the ambiguity of Gay's attitude comes not from perception of the essential humanity of his victims but from pleasure in the wit of the malicious gossip he evokes.

> *Laura* learnt caution at too dear a cost.
> What Fair could e'er retrieve her honour lost?
> Secret she loves; and who the nymph can blame,
> Who durst not own a footman's vulgar flame?
> (11. 49-52)

The tone of pretended sympathy and interest is precisely captured; and, although we recognize it perfectly, nothing in Gay's poem forces us to take it seriously.

To be sure, the real targets of satire in "The Tea-Table" are the subjects of the dialogue: Sylvia, the coquette, portrayed by Doris; and Laura, the prude, whom Melanthe describes. But the very form of the poem militates against taking the condemnation of Sylvia and Laura seriously, for that condemnation is uttered not in the poet's own voice but in the speech of two representatives of city life who are surely as corrupt as the women they criticize. The obvious enjoyment with which these two massacre reputations, the frivolity with which they speak, even the frivolity of their hypocrisy at the end of the poem (their two victims arrive, to be treated as bosom friends)—all these counteract tonally the seriousness of the indictment they present.

The entire poem depicts a society of almost total corruption. Sven Armens remarks, of the mock-pastoral form employed, that it "was meant to condemn the vices of the town, not by posing the contrast of a simple Golden Age, but by depicting directly the vicious manners of urban society in a form fraught with the associations of peace, virtue, and innocence." [10] Yet to depict these worldly maidens as urban shepherdesses, to parody the conventional pastoral dialogue so that instead of the usual pattern of two shepherds exchanging praise of their loved ones we have two women exchanging slander of their rivals (rivals, of course, only in the general sense that all women in this world are rivals of one another)—these reversals function also, quite simply, as jokes. If the jokes are potentially fraught with bitterness, their bitterness is not exploited; it remains in the realm of implication. The tone of "The Tea-Table" is close to that of a husband who enjoys complaining about his wife's maliciousness, while always assuming that such malice is inevitable in women and therefore excusable. The force of any criticism the eclogue may imply is vitiated by the personalities through whom criticism is conveyed. Once more, the satiric intention which may have motivated the poem seems almost to have been filtered out; once more the poet has failed to define for himself any clear position from which to condemn.

With a subject more obviously serious, dealing with ambiguity of feeling which comes close to hypocrisy, "The Funeral," the third of the town eclogues, is more firmly controlled by satiric purpose. But it, too, ultimately seems something quite different from satire. Sabina and Lucy, mistress and maid, are the characters, with an off-stage lover named Myrtillo. Sabina's husband, Fidelio, has been dead for two months; Sabina, in deepest mourning for him, dwells on his past virtues and refuses to entertain the overtures of Myrtillo. Lucy, a maid skilled in all the intrigues of love ("Her ready tongue, in secret service try'd,/ With equal fluency spoke truth or ly'd"; [11. 13-14]), delivers a letter from the would-be lover, which is immediately rejected. The rejection insists nominally on established standards of rectitude, but the sanctions invoked soon make it clear that the rectitude is only superficial:

> May Fops of mine, as *Flavia's,* favours boast,
> And Coquets triumph in my honour lost;
> May cards employ my nights, and never more
> May these curst eyes behold a Matadore!
> Break *China,* perish *Shock,* die *Perroquet!*
> When I *Fidelio's* dearer love forget.
> (11. 29-34)

This is the world of "The Rape of the Lock"; its standards, its references, its interests are almost precisely the same. Sabina's values are essentially those of Doris and Melanthe, the malicious gossipmongers of "The Tea-Table," but she is more interesting than they because her very hypocrisy demonstrates her awareness of a superior realm of values. Lucy will not allow her to pretend to moral superiority; when Sabina refers to Fidelio's wit, beauty, and virtue, the maid observes,

> Yet when he liv'd, he wanted ev'ry grace;
> That easy air was then an aukward pace:
> Have not your sighs in whispers often said,
> His dress was slovenly, his speech ill-bred?
> (11. 41-44)

Like her mistress, Lucy invokes sanctions which call to mind the larger patterns of the society she inhabits:

> Sooner shall Cits in fashions guide the Court,
> And Beaus upon the busy *Change* resort;
> Sooner the nation shall from snuff be freed,
> And Fops apartments smoke with India's weed,
> Sooner I'd wish and sigh through nunn'ry grates,
> Than recommend the flame *Sabina* hates.
> (11. 55-60)

More than any other of the town eclogues, "The Funeral" insists explicitly on maintaining the reader's consciousness of the nature of the world which makes such individuals meaningful. Its ultimate lack of satiric success comes from a certain confusion about the interpersonal relations involved. What, precisely, is the function of the maid in this interchange? Sometimes she seems devil's advocate, arguing for fickleness; sometimes she speaks for honesty, insisting that her mistress face the reality of her own emotions. Certainly the two roles are closely related, but the maid's motivation remains unclear. Does she express her mistress's real feelings? If so, she seems hardly needed in the dramatic structure of the poem: Sabina could go through the same process of rationalization in soliloquy.

A more convincing interpretation is that Sabina and Lucy both express genuine *parts* of Sabina's attitude, that Sabina really wants in some sense to be faithful to the memory of her husband, partly because of what people will think of her ("how loud would censure rail!/So soon to quit the duties of the veil!" [11. 103-4]), but partly from genuine feeling. Lucy convinces her of the validity of a mode of action that she also really desires, but her clinging to the alternative mode is not merely hypocrisy although it does, of course, partake of hypocrisy. The fact that the poem is a dialogue rather than a monologue creates ambiguities about the motivation, leaves open the possibility that Sabina is not entirely bad—that she represents yet one more case of a human being whose genuine feelings are corrupted by the evils of her society. The tone of sympathy has still not entirely disappeared; it is even stronger in the Quaker eclogue, "The Espousal," which deals with the justification of illicit love by religious convention, a subject which had been suggested by Swift in 1716.[11]

But the note of sympathy is almost entirely absent from "The Birth of the Squire," an energetic and compelling piece of satire, of which James Sutherland has written: "We might have expected this Hogarthian poem to figure prominently in anthologies, if anthologies were not so often compiled with an eye to the young and timid."[12] This eclogue seems dominated by a new singleness of purpose; its clear superiority to the other eclogues helps to clarify the satiric weaknesses of the town eclogues.

No named spokesman conveys the satiric message. Instead, the poet speaks in a voice of uncharacteristic authority which suggests his great debt to Virgil. The imitation of Virgil's fourth eclogue, which Gay suggests by his subtitle, is by no means close in detail after the first few lines; the important imitation is tonal. Gay has managed to capture something of Virgil's extraordinary combination of dignity and speed; he etches a swift and vivid portrait, and the sureness of his tone conveys his judgment and involves the reader in it. For this sureness, of course, Virgil cannot be entirely responsible; clearly something in the subject matter of this poem enabled Gay to write with more conviction than he characteristically mustered.

This eclogue deals directly with the country without the ambiguities created by the parodic structure of *The Shepherd's Week*. The Virgilian model is here used in far more straightforward and conventional fashion—to insist constantly on the deterioration of values between the classical past and the degraded present. Most of the poem's many ironies depend upon this implicit contrast:

> With frothy ale to make his cup o'er-flow,
> Barley shall in paternal acres grow;
> The bee shall sip the fragrant dew from flow'rs,
> To give metheglin for his morning hours;
> For him the clustring hop shall climb the poles,
> And his own orchard sparkle in his bowles.
> (11. 19-29)

The perversion of standards involved in turning agricultural activity toward the end of drunkenness is one of the most significant perversions in the poem: the squire's role as drinker is at least as important as his role as hunter. Hunting and drinking are his only real functions although he goes through the motions of others. The news of his birth, which "alarms the waking morn" (1. 7), foretells destruction for all "beasts of chase" (1. 9) and prophetically reddens the noses of the tenants with October ale (11. 13-14). The boy is educated by hearing the "monstrous tales" (1. 26) of his father's hunting exploits, tales which seem the more monstrous when one realizes that they are merely lies which the boy will some day tell his own son (11. 39-40). Such tales comprise the only education of the rural aristocracy; the boy could hardly be expected to endure the formal discipline of schools:

> Let younger brothers o'er dull authors plod,
> Lash'd into *Latin* by the tingling rod;
> No, let him never feel that smart disgrace:
> Why should he wiser prove than all his race?
> (11. 45-48)

For this is indeed the degradation of a race, not merely of an individual; one source of strength in the poem is Gay's constant perception of his victim not at all as an individual, simply as a horrifying and thoroughly representative type of modern corruption. Through perceiving the squire steadily as a type rather than as a human being, Gay escapes the temptation of sympathy, is enabled really to wield the satirist's lash without feeling that no specific person should be blamed for faults derived from the social structure. In this poem he seems to see what Pope always saw: the evils of the social structure grow from the corruption of individuals as well as vice versa.

Twice in the poem Gay, using the assured and authoritative tone appropriate to his role as wise man and satirist, addresses the squire directly: once to criticize his passion for hunting, again to rebuke him for his love of drink. In both instances an ironic sequel immediately suggests how futile such attempts at education must necessarily be. The warning about hunting occurs immediately after Gay's account of a hunting accident:

> O ventr'ous youth, thy thirst of game allay,
> Mayst thou survive the perils of this day!
> He shall survive; and in late years be sent
> To snore away Debates in *Parliament*.
> (11. 73-76)

To "reform" this squire must be meaningless; if he gives up hunting, he is capable of no more significant activity. His final public role, the poet then explains, is justice of the peace; he cares only to punish poachers, to preserve the game for his own butchery.

The warning about drinking is more extensive, and seems more seriously offered; it leads directly into the powerful concluding passage of the poem:

> O where is wisdom, when by this [liquor] o'erpower'd?
> The State is censur'd, and the maid deflower'd!
> And wilt thou still, O Squire, brew ale so strong?
> Hear then the dictates of prophetic song.
> Methinks I see him in his hall appear,
> Where the long table floats in clammy beer,
> 'Midst mugs and glasses shatter'd o'er the floor,
> Dead-drunk his servile crew supinely snore;
> Triumphant, o'er the prostrate brutes he stands,
> The mighty bumper trembles in his hands;
> Boldy he drinks, and like his glorious Sires,
> In copious gulps of potent ale expires.
>
> (11. 97-108)

This vision of the final degradation deriving from the squire's birth—implicitly contrasted with Virgil's vision of a Golden Age, of salvation brought by the child whose birth he celebrates—glows with utter conviction. The poet apparently feels no need to explain or justify himself; his language is unqualified, both in its ironies ("his glorious Sires," such modifiers as "boldly" and "triumphant") and in its direct condemnation ("his servile crew supinely snore"; "the prostrate brutes"). He offers without further comment an image of triumph so totally distorted as to become pure horror. In its final passage and throughout, "The Birth of the Squire" consistently demonstrates restraint of this sort, and total commitment.

John Gay may have been confused in his attitudes toward the city and its values, but he clearly feels no confusion about one evil of the country: corruption in the upper classes. He is far more tolerant of over-indulgence among the peasantry: consider his attitude toward the drunkenness of Bowzybeus in "Saturday" *(The Shepherd's Week),* where his tone is affectionate, indulgent:

> the giddy clown
> Again upon a wheat-sheaf drops adown;
> The pow'r that guards the drunk, his sleep attends,
> 'Till, ruddy, like his face, the sun descends.
>
> ("Saturday," 11. 125-28)

The peddlar may be nothing but a "giddy clown," but he is associated with nature, guarded by mysterious powers, laughed at for being ludicrous, but not criticized for being corrupt. He is, after all, behaving quite naturally; no more can be demanded. The squire, on the other hand, has a comparatively exalted heritage and responsibilities; his failure to live up to heritage or responsibilities is significantly ugly, an appropriate symbol for the ugliness of modern life as compared with ancient. Gay despises him, and feels no qualms about his feelings; he judges the aristocrat and the country bumpkin by entirely different standards and is quite secure in doing so. "Lilies that fester smell far worse than weeds": the degradation of the squire is so complete, and so appalling, that Gay seems hardly to consider him human at all. His attitude toward the squire is close to that he manifests toward some of the symbolic animal figures in the *Fables*, and this fact is a meaningful source of strength in what is clearly the best of the eclogues.

The final major class of poems in the 1720 volume is the tale. Examination of the tales increases one's sense of Gay's essential purposelessness up to this time, his inability to settle finally on themes or techniques most congenial to him. There are five of the little versified stories, four of them ribald, none with more than isolated moments of poetic merit. The ribald ones are all anti-Catholic in bias, depending largely on jokes about the bawdiness and corruption of the Catholic clergy; they are pseudo-Chaucerian in tone and, in one case, in language. The jokes are weak, the structure flabby; only an occasional couplet strikes the characteristic Gay note. "The Mad-Dog" is certainly the cleverest, if also the bawdiest, of the tales; it extends its implications explicitly beyond the dirty joke it depends on to draw analogies between the lecherous woman and such other images of social corruption as the extortionist, the courtier, and the scandalmonger. In the other instance where Gay attempts to extend a moral, "A True Story of an Apparition," he is far less successful. The tale is an old-fashioned ghost story, not particularly ingenious, but rich in the paraphernalia of horror. Ghosts, however, seemed less acceptable to Gay than bawdry. Although he begins the tale with insistence on the reality of ghosts, he ends by declaring it was all a dream, designed to illustrate the futility of "the statesman's vast ambitious scheme" (1. 139). His lack of sureness is illustrated once more.

Up to 1725, then (the date of the epistle "To a Lady on her

Passion for Old China"), Gay had not clearly found his way. We have not considered all his minor poems, which include serious pieces ("A Contemplation on Night," "A Thought on Eternity," etc.); songs ("Damon and Cupid," "Daphne and Chloe"); translations from Ovid and Ariosto; and one famous ballad ("Sweet William's Farewell to Black-ey'd Susan")—but few of them seem, in poetic merit, worthy of detailed consideration. On the whole, they intensify one's sense of a poet groping to find his proper mode. But it is possible, on the basis of what Gay had written thus far, to speculate on what his proper mode might be. If he attempts satire—and certainly his inclinations seem to run strongly in this direction—he must find subject matter about which he feels perfectly committed, and a technique which will enable him to deal with it without allowing his sympathy for all fellow human beings to get in his way. He was to discover both in writing the *Fables*.

CHAPTER 4

Man and Beast

IN 1727, after his experimentation with such diverse modes as verse epistles, songs, and versified tales, Gay published a first series of *Fables,* returning thus to a well-defined, highly formalized tradition and achieving new satiric vigor and clarity. Except for *The Beggar's Opera,* nothing he wrote was to bring him comparable fame. The *Fables* solidified his reputation. They were well-known and seldom criticized among his contemporaries, who "quoted from them and referred to them without stopping to estimate their quality." [1] Yet, as James Sutherland notes, the fables, "once so popular," are "now hardly read at all." [2] They have gone through more than 350 editions, including translations into Urdic and Bengali,[3] to become virtually unknown today—despite the fact that they help to define Gay at his very best.

As recently as 1939, however, a modern critic and poet suggested an interesting possible explanation of the disrepute into which these tales have fallen. Henry W. Wells published in the *Sewanee Review* a long poem in heroic couplets about various eighteenth-century satirists. In it, Gay appears (as a spirit) and speaks for himself (less deftly, it must be said, than he spoke during his life):

> General the terms wherewith I damned mankind,
> So thin the weapon, they could scarcely find
> The place at which the sabre entered in
> And many thought them wounded by a pin
> Who after saw their folly fully known
> And all their ills by my incision shown.[4]

It is true that the fables are deceptively unpretentious as a whole; one can easily skim their surface, accepting the explicit morals they sometimes offer, without being in the least disturbed by any sharpness or aware of complexities frequently lurking in the depths. A contemporary comment, also in verse, suggests how comfortably the fables were accepted in their own time. Writing in the *London Magazine* (February, 1737), one "R.D." observes of Gay:

> His solid lines the taste must suit
> Of ev'ry thing, except *a brute.*
> E'en brutes 'emselves his art can teach
> To talk, to argue;—nay, to preach.
> Judicious guide of slipp'ry youth!
> Ingenious fictions full of truth!
> Emblems divine, of human woe! . . .

It is quite clear that the author of these couplets believes Gay to be an impeccable moralist whose verses were universally pleasing—except, of course, to "brutes." "R.D." would have been surprised to read Duncan Tovey's comments a century and a half later on Gay's fables: "The main purpose of his *menagerie* is to depreciate man; and a curious and sympathetic reader, who should take Gay seriously, would discover that the only animal upon whom man can look down from a higher moral elevation is—of all creatures in the world—the turkey. Gay belongs to a fashionable school, in which there was but one sincere professor; and even the terrible earnestness of Swift was as powerless as the affectation of the rest to disturb the latent satisfaction of humanity." [5]

Of course any utterance by a Victorian critic about an eighteenth-century poet is likely to strike that note of scorn; what is interesting in Tovey's pronouncement is not his assessment of merit but his version of the content of the fables. From his point of view, as from Wells' (with, of course, a very different value judgment attached), Gay's tales are fiercely satiric, strongly condemnatory. Yet "R.D." provides testimony (and Irving's biography offers abundant corroboration) that Gay's contemporaries found the fables perfectly innocuous.

It is clear that, whatever his purposes, Gay worked hard on the fables. "Though this is a kind of writing that appears very easy," he wrote to Swift, "I find it the most difficult of any that I ever undertook." [6] The first series contained fifty poems, most of them quite short. But they are closely packed and highly polished; they demonstrate far greater control than anything Gay had written before. By using animals (and sometimes inanimate objects or classical deities) as characters instead of people, the poet gained an automatic distance from his subject which greatly encouraged satiric clarity. Joseph Warton complained that Gay's fables were weak in "ascribing to the different animals and objects introduced speeches and actions inconsistent with their several natures."[7] Elephants, he thought, had nothing to do with booksellers' shops; to place such a creature in such an environment was ridiculous.

But such incongruities provide almost a central principle for many of the fables, and an extremely valuable device for Gay's purposes. To use characters who were solely images, having as little to do with the real nature of animals as with the full nature of human beings, was a protection against his own tendency to sympathize with his victims, to perceive them too completely and consequently be unable to condemn them, to be aware of too many possibilities. Given the genre of fable, the possibilities become controllable: the creator of the characters can make them act precisely as he chooses because they have no innate principle of action, being neither human nor essentially animal.

Of course a long tradition of beast fables existed: translations of Aesop were abundant and popular in the eighteenth century, and so were adaptations of Aesop's technique to comment on contemporary events. There was a long native tradition as well, in folktale and more sophisticated literary forms. Reynard the Fox was a familiar character; Chaucer had used Chaunticleer and Pertelote, a rooster and hen, as comic characters in the "Nun's Priest's Tale"; children, then as now, loved fairy tales in which foxes and hens and geese and wolves outsmart one another. In part, Gay inherited a well-defined collection of type characters: the wily fox, the vain rooster, the owl who appears wise but is stupid. But he also created his own types: the elephant in the bookseller's shop is a good instance of the verve and whimsy with which he did so. In all of his best fables the reader senses clearly the poet's delight in his own fancies. Such qualities—verve, whimsy, fancifulness, delight—may obscure for the unwary reader the intensity of the fables' satiric thrust; the surface lightness of these pieces disguises their deep seriousness.

But how to define that seriousness? When one reads the fifty first fables in sequence, a sense of pattern gradually emerges. Although the individual poems use differing techniques and deal with different problems, they seem thematically and tonally unified. The nature of their unity may be suggested by the elephant fable to which Warton objected, a piece fully representative of Gay at his best which points to many of his central concerns in the fables.

Fable X, called "The Elephant and the Bookseller," begins with a mock-serious introduction about the fantastic tales of travel writers:

> The man, who with undaunted toils
> Sails unknown seas to unknown soils,
> With various wonders feasts his sight:
> What stranger wonders does he write!
> We read, and in description view
> Creatures which *Adam* never knew;
> For, when we risque no contradiction,
> It prompts the tongue to deal in fiction.
> Those things that startle me or you,
> I grant are strange; yet may be true.
> (ll. 1-10)

These lines, wonderfully ambiguous in their point of view, afford an ideal introduction to the tale which follows. Gay suggests alternately the attitude of the traveler and that of the reader, but neither the traveler's attitude nor the reader's is itself a constant. The traveler is undaunted, heroic, a seer of wonders—yet the wonders he writes about are stranger than those he sees, and the implication is clear that he deals in fiction rather than fact. On the other hand, just when one is tempted to assume that nothing a traveler writes is to be believed, Gay switches his perspective to insist that, no matter how strange the wonders depicted, they "may be true." What, then, are we expected to think about his little tale? He quotes, in Chaucerian fashion, various authorities for the sagacity of elephants, ending with Pliny to attest their learning; then he produces his own account of a Greek-reading pachyderm.

The elephant is rummaging in a bookseller's shop, "Not like our modern dealers, minding/Only the margin's breadth and binding" (11. 25-26), but carefully contemplating the contents of the volumes he encounters. He comes across a book which attempts to define the natures of all animals and birds, and comments on what he finds there:

> Man with strong reason is endow'd;
> A Beast scarce [instinct] is allow'd:
> But let this author's worth be try'd,
> 'Tis plain that neither was his guide.
> Can he discern the diffrent natures,
> And weigh the pow'r of other creatures,
> Who by the partial work hath shown
> He knows so little of his own?
> (11. 35-42)

The spaniel is depicted as fawner and flatterer, yet man himself, particularly in the courts of kings, is a flatterer and fawner from whom "a spaniel still might learn" (1. 48). The fox is censured as a thief and a plunderer, but the fox too could improve his dexterity by studying the "courtiers tricks, and lawyers arts" (1. 51). Lion, wolf, and tiger are cursed for bloodthirstiness: "But is not man to man a prey?/Beasts kill for hunger, men for pay" (11. 55-56). Finally the bookseller, impressed by the presence of a Greek-reading elephant, addresses him:

> Learn'd Sir, if you'd employ your pen
> Against the senseless sons of men,
> Or write the history of *Siam*,
> No man is better pay than I am;
> Or, since you're learn'd in *Greek*, let's see
> Something against the Trinity.
> (11. 61-66)

The wise elephant refuses: "Leave man on man to criticise" (1. 70), he observes, remarking that

> Envy's a sharper spur than pay,
> No author ever spar'd a brother,
> Wits are game-cocks to one another.
> (11. 74-76)

The effects here are extremely complicated and, as usual in Gay, difficult to define. The clearest "moral" is that animals are superior to men, a point frequently suggested in the fables.

The introductory discussion of the validity of travelers' tales, however, with its insistence on ambiguity (the tales may be true or fiction—Gay commits himself to neither position) brings up the question of what the reader's attitude toward this particular tale should be. Of course in one sense the fable is complete fiction—no elephant ever inhabited a bookseller's shop, and Gay does not expect his readers to believe in this one. But are we to believe the elephant's judgments on men, to accept his authority as moral arbiter? Does he demonstrate himself to be as superior to men as he asserts himself to be? In reply to the bookseller's overtures he wrinkles "with a sneer his trunk" (1. 67), accusing the man of drunkenness. That sneer is pure comedy, the characteristic comedy of these fables. Gay remembers what animals look like, is aware of the ludicrousness of the situations into which he forces them, provides the sharp visual perception which reminds the reader of that ludicrousness. Our sense of the elephant's comic aspect derives partly from an assumption of human superiority to animals: a sneering elephant is funny because it is the prerogative of human beings to sneer; the elephant merely apes the manners of his betters. Or is he aping his inferiors? The joke is complex; the elephant, with his vivid sense of superiority to men, imitates humanity in one of its more unattractive aspects. Moreover, his final condemnation of mankind reveals his partial acceptance of human standards: he degrades man by comparing him to a member of the animal kingdom ("Wits are game-cocks to one another"). The elephant's position is not totally clear-cut; neither is the proper attitude of the reader.

The bookseller, the poem's only representative of humanity, is clearly the butt. His immediate reaction ("what a genius have I found!" [1. 59]) is exactly right, quite convincingly human. His immediate willingness to betray his fellowmen in order to profit from the anti-human tract of an elephant, his enterprise in thinking of the history of Siam as a proper subject for an elephant pen, his imagination in realizing that he might even hope for "Something against the Trinity"—these reactions supply the rapid series of comic touches so characteristic of these poems, and they demonstrate and emphasize the unscrupulousness and treachery of men. The indictment of mankind provided by the bookseller as representative is more convincing and perhaps more biting than that offered by the elephant as dispassionate observer. But the bookseller's central flaw is surprisingly close to the elephant's weakness. Entrepreneur though he is, this merchant is not a vicious man; his treachery and unscrupulousness are effects rather than causes of his commercial enterprise. His commercial enterprise simply *blinds* him to other considerations; because of his interest in making money he cannot be aware of moral concerns.

It is exactly such blindness, of course, that the elephant originally accuses mankind of: he condemns the author of the animal book for his "partial work"—partial in two senses: biased and incomplete. But the elephant, too, has a limited perspective; he sees life only from an elephant's point of view, as the commercial man sees it from the commercial man's point of view and as all men see only from the human point of view. It takes a god to laugh at such universal limitations of perspective, and this is exactly the point: Gay manages in these fables to assume, for the first time, the removed, godlike perspective and authority of the assured satirist. Perhaps because such a viewpoint, such authority, did not come naturally to him, limitation of perspective seems the central theme of the first group of fables. It is rarely, to be sure, the *nominal* theme: the episode of the elephant is characteristic in this respect as in so many others. It seems to concern issues much simpler than this question of perspective, inevitably so replete with ambiguities—for what, indeed, is "proper" perspective on any human situation? This problem never troubles Gay; most of these first fables seem further glosses on the contention that "life is a jest and all things show it." Over and over the poet reveals how ludicrous is man's self-importance; over and over he insists only human blindness can conceivably explain human pride. It is a good eighteenth-century theme: Pope's "Essay on Man" states it most emphatically, usually in non-satiric terms. And it is a theme for which images from the animal kingdom are particularly appropriate, with their constant implicit reminder that man is, after all, placed in the Great Chain of Being *just* above the animals, that to avoid sliding into pure animality requires ceaseless effort. Gay employs animal images, interspersing them with human embodiments of the same point; the cumulative effect of the first fifty fables derives largely from the insistent restatement, in radically different terms, of the single truth that all creatures are fatally blind in some significant respect, and that pride and vanity are the sources of blindness. This truth may be concealed by the explicit statement of some other, less fundamental, "point"; but almost always it lurks beneath the surface. It is perhaps for this reason that some careful readers of Gay's fables have found them unexpectedly disturbing.

One of his most explicit statements of his central theme is in Fable XVIII, "The Painter Who Pleased No body and Every body." That this tale troubled at least one reader is attested by an exceptionally interesting series of "Letters on Gay's Fables" which appeared in the *European Magazine* in 1816. The author is identified as being also the writer of *Fables for the Fire-Side;* it is presumably from the point of view of the conventional fabulist that he condemns Gay so fiercely. His objections are largely irrational, but all point to significant truths about Gay's fables: the critic has clearly felt some of the complexity of these tales, even though he tries to reduce it to merely a new form of simplicity. Fable XVIII, for example, is superficially easy to summarize: it relates the career of an exceptionally talented portrait painter who has the knack of capturing his subjects' precise appearance on canvas. Gradually he loses his friends, his practice, and his money: nobody wants such portraits. Then he supplies himself with a bust of Venus and one of Apollo, paints all his subjects by one model or the other, is universally praised, and raises his prices. The complaint of the fireside fabulist is that this tale is "double-faced," that it favors vice as well as virtue: successful flattery by the painter can only encourage others to do likewise.[8]

Of course, in a very complicated sense, this is precisely the point of the tale: it is only surprising that no critic before 1816 had noticed in print how singularly ambiguous was the moral application of many of Gay's fables. But Gay's clear recognition that the painter is following the "best" possible course for a man in society finally intensifies the rich moral statement of his poem. This tale, like the one about the elephant, begins with a preamble about the difficulty a story teller finds in being believed: the traveler who wishes to be credited must always "Keep probability in view" (l. 2). There is one exception, Gay continues, to this general rule:

> flatt'ry never seems absurd,
> The flatter'd always takes your word,
> Impossibilities seem just,
> They take the strongest praise on trust;
> Hyperboles, though ne'er so great,
> Will still come short of self-conceit.
> (11. 7-12)

Awareness that reference to the difficulties of being a poet is at least subterranean in the tale is important in understanding its moral effect. Gay's own solution to the problem of artistic honesty is precisely the opposite of the painter's. Gay chooses to take the satirist's position, to make his criticism ever sharper and more exact, rather than, like the painter, to retreat from the struggle. The poem insists, however, that the satirist's solution is not socially acceptable, for popular success must depend on falsification. And it makes this point without bitterness, with some of Gay's familiar sympathy for the weak world of humanity. (It is significant that he deals in this tale directly with man, not with man in the guise of some animal.) When the lord has his portrait painted and sees the resulting painting of Apollo, he reacts first with protest: "Dear sir, for me, it's far too young" (1. 50). The artist replies that in such matters "we painters must decide" (1. 52); he convinces his subject, of course, but there is pathos in the conviction: "My lord examin'd it anew;/No looking-glass seem'd half so true" (11. 55-56). The poem's summary couplet intensifies one's vague sense of sympathy: "when thus happily he wrought,/Each found the likeness in his thought" (11. 67-68).

The painter is, in other words, appealing to the universal—almost the defining—human weakness: the gap that exists between one's image of oneself and actuality. It is unfortunate that there should be such gaps, but it is also pathetic, and Gay—even as satirist—is aware of both facts. The poem implies criticism of a society based on human weakness rather than strength, but not criticism of individual members of that society. The 1816 critic was quite right in feeling that the painter is not condemned for his acceptance of the convenient, the efficient means of making money. One must recognize him as weak, to be sure, but the real evil is social, not individual. That an alternative procedure is possible for the artist, the poem itself attests, but alternatives are difficult. Gay does not make his morality seem either easy or simple in the best of his fables; this fact is one important source of the strength of the fables.

The theme of human blindness produced by vanity and pride could be expressed also through animal images. Fable XIV, for example, "The Monkey who had Seen the World," tells of a tame monkey who learns the evils of court life and then escapes to transmit them to his fellow-monkeys. He invites his companions to "Reform your state, and copy me" (1. 42) in all forms of human corruption; with no genuine standards to oppose to these, the monkeys agree and become as evil as men. Once more, the root evil is limited perspective, in this case from limited experience. "The Old Woman and her Cats," Fable XXIII, shows a hag complaining that she is thought a witch because she keeps cats; the cats, with a different but equally limited point of view, reply that they lose credit, on the contrary, because of their association with her. "The Butterfly and the Snail," Fable XXIV, depicts the pride of a butterfly who has forgotten its origins; a snail finally reminds him that he is basically a caterpillar after all. Turkeys complain that the chief sin of man is gluttony; an ant who has just escaped the turkey's beak makes the obvious comment that it is all a matter of point of view (Fable XXXVIII). Two monkeys at a fair interpret what they see as the attempts of humanity to imitate them (Fable XL). An owl explains that all birds admire him, and that man demonstrates his limitations by failing to understand the profundity of owls (Fable XLI); or horses interpret the universe as being one in which men serve them (Fable XLIII); or fleas tell man that he was made only for their need (Fable XLIX). The entire natural universe demonstrates Gay's point, and he makes that point without wavering. Lack of self-knowledge is everywhere manifest; analysis of it must touch everyone.

With such unity of theme, how do these fables avoid monotony? The tale of the horses' rationalization and that of the flea's, for example, are essentially identical and a reader will recognize this fact. Even so, he is not likely to be bored: the variations, the disguises, are themselves interesting. The animal characters are not always, as in the typical fable, images for different sorts of men. Sometimes, on the contrary, an explicit separation between the world of animals and that of men is insisted upon.

When such a separation exists, it is usually not flattering to men: animals are perceived as antagonists of, and usually as moral superiors to, human beings. The elephant, for example, feels his superiority keenly; if we are not quite so willing as he is to accept his relative uprightness, at least the fable offers no evidence to shift the weight to the other side: one can hardly believe the bookseller wiser or more moral than the elephant. Fable V, "The Wild Boar and the Ram," energetic and economical in construction, presents a vision of obscure justice operating in the universe to justify and regulate the antagonism between men and animals. It begins with a "pathetic" image:

> Against an elm a sheep was ty'd,
> The butcher's knife in blood was dy'd;
> The patient flock, in silent fright,
> From far beheld the horrid sight. . . .
> (11. 1-4)

The conventionality of the language ("patient flock," "horrid sight") reassures us that no special reaction is demanded. The issue becomes moral rather than sentimental when a "savage Boar" (1. 5) standing nearby mocks "the fleecy brood" (1. 6) for their cowardice in failing to take revenge on the men who treat them so cruelly. A ram replies that the sheep's revenge is of a subtle kind:

> Know, Those who violence pursue
> Give to themselves the vengeance due,
> For in these massacres they find
> The two chief plagues that waste mankind.
> Our skin supplys the wrangling bar,
> It wakes their slumbring sons to war,
> And well revenge may rest contented,
> Since drums and parchment were invented.
> (11. 21-28)

A sharp change of feeling is demanded of the reader in the course of these few lines. The initial sentimental vignette prepares us to offer easy, temporary sympathy to the suffering sheep. When the boar's voice intervenes, however, it seems perfectly logical: we are willing to believe, in terms of the fairy tale world of the fable, that sheep deserve vengeance if they are capable of taking it. And to whatever extent we have any reaction at all to the problems of these highly improbable animals, we participate in the boar's scorn for sheepish passivity. "The heart that wants [lacks] revenge is base," cries the boar (1. 14); we recognize and readily approve the accents of conventional heroism. Sheep are, after all, emblems of the eternal victim—a "fleecy brood," destined to be sheared and slaughtered.

But the poetic justice of the denouement requires a shift of perspective about values as well as about the place of sheep in the universe. The "patience" of the sheep, established in the third line and emphasized by the tone of the ram's utterance, so different from the boar's rabble-rousing vehemence, has its ultimate effect in furthering the impatience and violence of mankind. Man's destructiveness is essentially its own punishment; sheep provide the instruments; the sheep's serenity is its own reward. The sheep—"silly sheep," as they are so often termed in pastorals—are, after all, the true wits: wits in conception and in expression. This is the joke of the poem, but also its "lesson." And the shock of reversed perspective extends to the reader, to whatever degree he finds himself participating, even temporarily, in the values of the boar.

Of course this entire discussion is misleading because it has proceeded as though we took the world revealed by the fable with perfect seriousness. Almost all the fables are difficult to explicate for precisely the same reason: it is hard to define just what our attitude *is* toward the world they offer. Certainly we are always aware of it as fictional, and as something of a joke; our feelings toward it must be colored by our recollection of animal stories read in childhood. We do not for a moment suspend our disbelief; never do we think, even briefly, that rams and boars can have conversations of this sort, or that Gay is saying anything about the real nature of rams and boars. Our reading must involve a complex process of translation and interpretation; the animals are always somehow allegorical equivalents for man, even when the fable deals with antagonisms between men and animals. Fables are primarily concerned with truth, not with characters; that Gay can manage along the way to make his characters come to life is testimony to his great skill in the genre.

Sheep are not the only animals revealed in these tales as morally superior antagonists to man. In Fable IX, "The Bull and the Mastiff," the bull kills the mastiff because the dog reveals that it has learned its values from a human butcher. (It is, of course, the ultimate, characteristic Gay irony that the bull, protesting human butchery, should act as butcher himself.) "The Philosopher and the Pheasant" (Fable XV) puts a philosopher in the position of realizing that he is hateful to all animals. Finally he overhears a mother pheasant explaining to her brood why man is the least trustworthy of animals: "In him ingratitude you find,/A vice peculiar to the kind" (11. 27-28). In a series of glosses on this text, she offers instances of human treachery: man's treatment of sheep, bees, and geese (after using the goose's quills for writing, finally "He takes the quills and eats the goose" [1. 42]). The poem's summary is, as usual, illuminating:

> Man then avoid, detest his ways,
> So safely shall prolong your days.
> When services are thus acquitted,
> Be sure we pheasants must be spitted.
> (11. 43-46)

Once more self-interest is finally dominant: the very fables which insist on man's moral inferiority to all other creatures demonstrate the extent to which animals share the vices they deplore. Nature is fallen as well as man; the fables leave one in no doubt about that fact. When a shepherd's dog encounters the wolf which has been ravaging his flock (Fable XVII, "The Shepherd's Dog and the Wolf"), the wolf explains that nature's fall is less serious than man's. He does not claim not to be a killer himself; he *does* claim that his killing is not so reprehensible as man's, for two reasons: wolves must eat, sheep are their natural food; and "A wolf eats sheep but now and then,/ Ten thousands are devour'd by men" (11. 31-32). Man's manifestations of self-interest are perverted, compared to those of the animals: self-interest itself may not be unnatural, but the ways in which it is indulged are. The implication is that the human pretense at moral superiority is most detestable of all—which leaves one with some questions about how one is to feel about Gay's world, in which *animals* insist on their moral superiority.

Perhaps the fullest explicit treatment in the fables of the precise relation between men and animals occurs in Fable XXXIII, "The Courtier and Proteus," where the courtier is enabled to capture the wily Proteus, a mythical sea deity who assumes various forms with miraculous rapidity, because no transformation can surprise one who is accustomed to the life at court. Proteus takes the form of a snake; the courtier remarks that, despite their pride, "All courtiers are of reptile race" (l. 26): they hiss with malice, gloat with envy, "And for convenience change their coat" (l. 30), shining with new luster though they have been born and bred on a dunghill. Proteus becomes a lion, a lynx, a wolf, an ass, a fox, a bear; the courtier insists that equivalents for all exist in his native environment, that courtiers "Down from the lyon to the ape,/Practise the frauds of ev'ry shape" (ll. 47-48). And, when he finally succeeds in capturing Proteus, he adds insult to injury by saying that courtiers are, after all, Proteus' superior: the courtier is "Not to be bound by any tyes,/And never forc'd to leave his lyes" (ll. 55-56).

This fable, thematically, justifies all the rest: given a world in which men practice the animal vices, made worse because they are presumably not natural to men (such, at any rate, seems to be Gay's assumption: as satirist he must believe that man is capable of reform, though tigers are not), tales of animal activities become singularly relevant to the human condition. And if the talking, thinking animals seem very much like men in disguise, so much the better; this is, after all, the point: man has made himself an animal. Many of the best fables deal with this notion, using animals as thinly disguised images of men. This fact was singularly disturbing to our critic of 1816, who referred to Fable XXIX, "The Fox at the Point of Death," as "nothing less than a temporary dereliction of his [Gay's] reason, and of all sense of religion, as well as of morality." [9]

The fable is simple, consisting mainly of the fox's deathbed speech to his children, which adjures them to depart from evil ways because "My crimes lye heavy on my heart" (l. 10). When he imagines the phantoms of slaughtered geese, turkeys, and chickens around him, his sons lick their lips for the feast, then reproach him for tempting them with the food of his imagination. Again the dying fox warns his progeny against evil, until one replies that foxes have such a bad name already it is useless to reform: any hen roost that is robbed will be blamed on them, for "A lost good name is ne'er retriev'd" (l. 46). Suddenly the feeble fox hears the cluck of a chicken and tells his sons to "Go, but be mod'rate in your food;/A chicken too might do me good" (11. 49-50). It is the argument of self-interest once more; and the central truth of the fable is that only self-interest has been working throughout. The old fox's argument against the murder of fowl has originated in his own lack of appetite: "All appetite had left his maw,/And age disarm'd his mumbling jaw" (11. 3-4). His appeal to his sons rest mainly on the notion that they will be safer if they give up plunder: "Does not the hound betray our peace,/And gins and guns destroy our race?" (11. 25-26). When they reply that they will not, in fact, be better off under such circumstances, he shifts ground completely; since his appetite has returned, his point of view has changed, and his argument for moderation is of precisely the same sort as his earlier plea for abstinence, based entirely on his personal desires and needs.

It is a mistake to assume that the old fox is a hypocrite; no hypocrisy is involved. He is both honest and consistent throughout. One of Gay's key insights is that such labels as "hypocrite" are all too readily applied; he argues implicitly throughout the fables for looking closely at various human activities in order to understand more fully the complexities of psychology.

Almost always the perceptions in these tales shed a comic light on man and his pretensions. If man is seen in the image of a fox, the stress is not on his skill in wiliness but on his pettiness of motivation. Frequently the metaphorical embodiments of human flaws have not even so much natural dignity: sparrows, geese, chickens, turkeys, pins and needles, even dunghills suggest various aspects of human nature. Limited perspective, Gay says, comes from pride; his sparrows and dunghills leave man little room to congratulate himself on his high place in the universe.

One of the most charming of the fables is "The Old Hen and the Cock" (Fable XX), which describes the human temptation to disobedience. The author of *Fables for the Fire-Side* concludes his attack on it by remarking that "a more ill-conducted, pernicious, or immoral fable, could not easily, if possibly, be written." [10] He is enraged because he feels that the fable is heretical as well as corrupting: the image of man it offers is all too close to the nature of fallen spirits who love evil for its own sake and desire to commit it simply because it is contrary to God's command (p. 120). Missing all Gay's ironies, the critic none the less calls the reader's attention to the real theological overtones of the poem.

The fable begins with what purports to be its moral: "Restrain your child; you'll soon believe/The text, which says, we sprung from *Eve*" (11. 1-2). The fable is announced, in other words, as being about the fallen nature of man. Its story is of a hen, one of whose chicks falls into a well and is drowned. Grief-stricken, she warns another of her sons, now a full-grown cock, to avoid the spot. The cock, as a natural consequence of the prohibition, is tempted to disobey; he hypothesizes that his mother doubts his courage, or alternatively, that she has stored treasure in that spot for her younger children. Finally he mounts the edge of the well, sees his reflection below, flies to the attack of the imaginary enemy, and is drowned, lamenting the while, "I ne'er had been in this condition/But for my mother's prohibition" (11. 47-48).

The 1816 critic accepts this comment at face value; he sees the fable as "an outrageous attempt to make our children believe that, if their parents lay restraints upon them, they will certainly experience an irresistible inclination to break through them";[11] he also comments that he has "not unfrequently heard this fable alluded to by refractory and ungovernable spirits as a defense of their bad conduct" (p. 121). It is a magnificent irony that the tale should be interpreted in this way—a perfect demonstration of its point; that men can rationalize any form of corruption into someone else's responsibility. This, as the fable seems to define it, *is* the fallen nature of man. And it is closely related to another human quality which the tale also demonstrates: pretentiousness, an outgrowth of that basic human flaw, pride. The poem's language emphasizes this quality, in both mother and son. The old hen grieves "all day" (1. 10) for her chick; the implication is clear that her grief will last only a day. When she sees the cock, affection suddenly grows in her heart; again there is a suggestion that it is a temporary—although not for that reason unreal—phenomenon. In the grip of this emotion, she speaks in an elevated fashion to her son:

let thy ever-wary tread
Avoid yon well; that fatal place
Is sure perdition to our race.
Print this my counsel on thy breast;
To the just Gods I leave the rest.
(11. 18-22)

Of course there is a simple joke in the mere fact of a hen's speaking in such tones, but the joke is not superficial. The elevation of the mother's speech is echoed in the son's thoughts: "Let courage female fears despise," he cries (1. 30), and his actual downfall is preceded by his announcing, "I stand resolv'd, and dare th' event" (1. 36). This is the language of heroism; it is used also for the description of his subsequent behavior:

He stretch'd his neck; and from below
With stretching neck advanc'd a foe;
With wrath his ruffled plumes he rears,
The foe with ruffled plumes appears;
Threat answer'd threat, his fury grew,
Headlong to meet the war he flew. . . .
(11. 39-44)

In other words, the precipitating cause of the cock's downfall is, once more, his false image of himself as hero: the blindness of vanity, the lack of self-knowledge characteristic of men—and in Gay's world, of animals—have been demonstrated again.

The reference to Eve suggests that this fable may be considered in a theological context; most of the fables in the first series can be thought of in the same way. For of course pride, presumption, vanity are all closely related, in Christian tradition, to original sin. Sven Armens is certainly right in characterizing Gay's attitude in these fables as essentially "neoclassical" and in this respect similar to that of the famous French fabulist, La Fontaine.[12] But the neoclassical attitude toward the position of man in the universe has strong affinities with the Christian attitude, as much of the modern controversy over the fourth book of *Gulliver's Travels* attests. Gay's Christian reference is particularly important because it emphasizes the extent to which, in these early fables, the poet is concerned with the essential nature of man rather than with specific and temporary faults. Although individual fables may appear to deal with individual weaknesses, the central issues involved are usually very fundamental indeed. "The Renaissance preoccupation with the terrible problem of man as beast or angel" [13] is the heart of the matter for Gay; and the fables, considered in the light of this problem, appear a good deal more penetrating and more profound than we may realize at first.

It is perhaps because Gay was concerned more with the basic problem of the nature of man than with individual weaknesses of man that so many of the most powerful fables in the first series offer no explicit moral at all, or only a brief one such as we saw in the episode of the cock and the hen. Often when a moral is explicitly presented, it is only the moral that the tale might have for the characters involved in it—not really the lesson that it offers for readers who are able to share even momentarily the satirist's removed perspective. Thus Fable IX, "The Bull and the Mastiff," an example of the way in which animals claim moral superiority to men in these tales, is prefaced with a moral statement about the desirability of having good preceptors for the training of youth. Fable XXII, "The Goat without a Beard," offers a moral in advance which is quite clearly intended to be undercut by the tale that follows:

> Excuse me, then; if pride, conceit
> (The manners of the fair and great)
> I give to monkeys, asses, dogs,
> Fleas, owls, goats, butterflys and hogs.
> I say, that these are proud. What then?
> I never said, they equal men.
>
> (11. 3-8)

But of course this disclaimer is partly ironic: although it is true enough that goats do not equal men in pride, yet the point of the fable is that the goat (like fleas, monkeys, asses) is an image for men; his whole significance depends upon this fact. Fable XLIV, "The Hound and the Huntsman," has a preliminary moral about the origins of impertinence. The story itself is, as usual, about pride and presumption—which are, to be sure, related to impertinence, but are far more important than it as subjects for the poet. Examples could easily be multiplied; this is a technique highly appropriate to Gay's vision of the human condition, for it plays its jokes upon the unwary reader and may cause him to realize most vividly the extent to which he is willing to rely upon unexamined assumptions and rationalizations.

An especially fine example of this technique in action is Fable XLV, "The Poet and the Rose," which offers the advance moral:

> I hate the man who builds his name
> On ruins of another's fame.
> Thus prudes by characters o'erthrown
> Imagine that they raise their own. . . .
> (11. 1-4)

Examples from the human realm continue; then Gay tells his story of a poet who wanders in the garden, plucks a rose, and extemporizes a pleasant little song in the seventeenth-century manner comparing the rose with his mistress. The second of its two verses is much to the disadvantage of the rose:

> Know, hapless flower, that thou shalt find
> More fragrant roses there;
> I see thy with'ring head reclin'd
> With envy and despair!
> One common fate we both must prove;
> You die with envy, I with love.
> (11. 25-30)

To this "an angry Rose" (1. 32) right out of *Through the Looking-Glass* offers a heated protest, pointing out that poets are dependent on roses for their imagery and asking:

> Does it to *Chloe's* charms conduce,
> To found her praise on our abuse?
> Must we, to flatter her, be made
> To wither, envy, pine and fade?
> (11. 37-40)

As a demonstration of the evils of invidious comparisons, this verse seems weak indeed; we can hardly be expected to take the rose's objections seriously. Our reasons for not taking them seriously may well be the true point of the poem. The rose's complaint seems ridiculous even on the symbolic level because we are conscious of the difference between poetic convention and literal fact, as the rose is not. The flower really is behaving precisely like her counterparts in *Through the Looking-Glass,* insisting, as they do, on the literalness of all language. ("'It says "Bough-wough!"' cried a Daisy: 'that's why its branches are called boughs!'") Yet the nature of such wit as this lyric employs, as Addision pointed out, is that its similitudes have little to do with actuality.[14] The fable could almost be a text on true versus false wit—and a text which relates such purely literary matters to the general theme of man's limited perspective. The rose's failure to make meaningful distinctions comes from a sort of self-obsession, an assumption that the self-esteem of roses is the most significant matter to be considered in any poetic treatment of flowers; it provides one more image of the distortions caused by vanity.

So, although the explicitly stated moral *is*, on an unemphatic level, demonstrated by the poem, the fable's strongest effect has to do with ideas which almost contradict the explicit moral. The poet perceives, and causes us to perceive, from a perspective which makes "fame" a relatively minor concern. The moral implications of his best fables are invariably complex; he is obviously wise in refraining from direct statement of them.

Conversely, when Gay succumbs to the temptation of stating a moral explicitly and then demonstrating it, his fables become both weak and tedious. Fable XXVIII, "The Persian, the Sun, and the Cloud," is a good example of a piece weakened by topical reference and limited moral. It begins with a highly conventional personification, through which the moral is conveyed:

> Is there a bard whom genius fires,
> Whose ev'ry thought the God inspires?
> When Envy reads the nervous lines,
> She frets, she rails, she raves, she pines,
> Her hissing snakes with venom swell,
> She calls her venal train from hell,
> The servile fiends her nod obey,
> And all *Curl's* authors are in pay.
> (11. 1-8)

The problem is not with the introduction but with the application which grows out of it. Gay's letter to Swift implies strongly that the morals preceded the tales in his conception of the fables and that this fact had much to do with his difficulty in writing them. This is hard to believe of most of the fables, but quite credible in this instance: the tale itself is of a Persian engaged in worshiping the sun and thus arousing the jealousy of a passing cloud. The cloud covers the sun with darkness and demands worship as more powerful than the "gawdy God" (1. 23) which he has obscured. Refusing the Persian insists that the cloud is but a passing thing, created by the god whom he worships. A wind rises, the cloud disappears, "The glorious orb the day refines,/Thus Envy breaks, thus Merit shines" (1. 37-38). The moral tag at the end supports the moral statement at the beginning; no further complexity has been provided. Although the moral is quite unexceptionable, it is made no more interesting by the fable which illustrates it: the characters are unconvincing, we find no moments of visual perception, no comic touches. The allegorical conception of sun and cloud is perceptive, but in the actual fable everything is on the same pedestrian level; no character is really more than an abstraction: these are not the qualities that won popularity for Gay's tales. But such weaknesses are characteristic only of relatively few tales (Fable XXXI, "The Universal Apparition," is another especially striking example), and these are invariably the ones in which preoccupation with the moral has interfered with the vividness of conception of the stories themselves.

This group of fables was dedicated to the boy prince, William, Duke of Cumberland:

> Accept, young *Prince,* the moral lay,
> And in these tales mankind survey;
> With early virtues plant your breast,
> The specious arts of vice detest.
>
> (Fable I, "The Lyon, the Tyger, and the Traveller," 11. 1-4)

One might expect, considering the dedication and the nominal purpose of the fables—to educate the prince in the nature and practice of virtue—that the poet would concern himself much more exclusively with the specific evils of the court. But—although such court vices as flattery and treachery are frequently emphasized, and the key vice of pride is one to which princes may be thought peculiarly susceptible—the great achievement of these poems is that they do not seem limited by their particular time or purpose. They achieve precisely the sort of universality that the introduction hints as a possibility:

> Thus ev'ry object of creation
> Can furnish hints to contemplation
> And from the most minute and mean
> A virtuous mind can morals glean.
> (Introduction, "The Shepherd and the Philosopher," 11. 69-72)

The universe is perceived throughout as a coherent and meaningful whole; the steadiness of Gay's vision informs and strengthens the whole first sequence of fables.

II

The second series of fables, published in 1738, six years after Gay's death, is completely different from the first in tone, emphasis, and technique. Only sixteen fables are included, but they occupy almost as much bulk as the original fifty. Each is specifically dedicated to someone, by name or by profession; all are much more precisely focused than those in the original group. Organized roughly alike, all begin with a lengthy moralistic preamble followed by a tale sometimes not so long as the introduction which it is clearly designed to support. The morals of these tales are quite different from most of those in the first group. Now the emphasis on state affairs seems almost obsessive. Over and over the same points are made: there is much corruption in the government; people at court care only for money, not for the welfare of the country; Gay himself is disinterested, uncorruptible, and consequently without power or place. Sven Armens argues convincingly that these tales were written at the time when Gay was becoming more closely allied with the Opposition Party, so that he could find "a focal point for his satire on false reason, an epitome of the townsman in the person of Sir Robert Walpole,"[15] the prime minister attacked directly also in *The Beggar's Opera.* Gay felt, Armens writes:

> that only a severe change in the moral attitude of individuals and a sincere transference of value aims away from the accumulation of wealth and power for self-aggrandizement, away from the absurd necessity of keeping in vogue, and away from the false distortions of natural impulses, would suffice to remedy . . . Augustan social evils. To effect such a change was certainly part of the poet's task according to any neoclassicist, but because of his connections with the Opposition Party members, Gay found it somewhat too easy to

believe that the roots of most of these evils could be laid to the misconduct of the Walpole government with its intimate court alliances. (190)

"Somewhat too easy" is perhaps the most appropriate critical designation for these fables. In comparison with the first group they have an automatic, predictable quality, intensified by their repetition of ideas and themes. Moreover, they are frequently marred by a note of smugness:

> Wherever those a people drain,
> And strut with infamy and gain,
> I envy not their guilt and state,
> And scorn to share the publick hate.
> Let their own servile creatures rise,
> By screening fraud and venting lyes:
> Give me, kind heav'n, a private station,
> A mind serene for contemplation,
> Title and profit I resign,
> The post of honour shall be mine.

(Fable II, "The Vultur, the Sparrow, and other Birds," ll. 63-72)

We can hardly quarrel with Gay's moral position here: his detestation of "guilt and state," his preference for privacy, serenity and honor, are admirable. Yet such verbal assurances can be made with the greatest facility; no doubt Walpole could have managed similar ones. The apparent assumption that a preference for virtue is synonymous with its possession is troublesomely naïve, and it runs through many of these poems. It has nothing to do with the godlike perspective of the satirist that we noted in the first series. Indeed, although the poet explicitly elevates himself above the level of those he attacks, the effect of his concern to remove himself is rather to suggest that he is quite as human as his victims, subject to the same temptations, to be judged by the same standards. The sense of authority so important to the first fables is all too frequently missing from the second group.

Yet we should not be too hard on these final sixteen tales. If they lack the special virtues of the first collection, they frequently have virtues of their own; they evidence—in sharp perceptions, in moments of insight, even in sustained sequences of passion—the skill of a mature poet. It is unfortunate only that this skill should be so often vitiated by the weaknesses of the immature amateur politician.

On the other hand, the passion that brings some interludes to life is usually specifically political; at times Gay can summon up an almost Popean control of colloquial language and rhythms to express his detestation of court corruption. A good example comes from the same poem as the passage quoted above to illustrate his distasteful smugness; it includes, indeed, the lines immediately preceding the sequence:

> All consciences must bend and ply,
> You must vote on, and not know why;
> Through thick and thin you must go on;
> One scruple, and your place is gone.
> Since plagues like these have curst a land,
> And fav'rites cannot always stand,
> Good courtiers should for change be ready,
> And not have principles too steady;
> For should a knave engross the power,
> (God shield the realm from that sad hour,)
> He must have rogues or slavish fools;
> For what's a knave without his tools?

(Fable II, "The Vultur, the Sparrow, and other Birds," 11. 51-62)

There is nothing fresh about this language; indeed, Gay relies largely on cliches: "all consciences must bend," "through thick and thin," the metaphor of the plague and the curse—none of these is startling or original. The points are understated: "not have principles too steady," "that sad hour" (rather than "disastrous" or "desperate" or some other more emphatic adjective); even the form of the last sentence seems deliberately to withhold emphasis. The passage's energy and conviction come partly from that very understatement, combined with the speed of the lines. One idea follows another with the greatest rapidity; the movement of the verse conveys directly the tumultuous movement from one unethical act to another which is its subject. The lack of decoration and elaboration suggests the poet's involvement in his ideas. Apparently concerned to communicate feeling as much as to make a point, he does both successfully.

Another skill manifested especially in these later fables is the ability to convey directly the precise quality of social life. Fable

XII, "Plutus, Cupid, and Time," spends a long preamble on the efforts of the socialite to kill time. They are much the same as the efforts of his equivalent today:

> What can one do? I rose at nine.
> 'Tis full six hours before we dine:
> Six hours! no earthly thing to do!
> Would I had doz'd in bed 'till two.
> A pamphlet is before him spread,
> And almost half a page is read;
> Tir'd with the study of the day,
> The flutt'ring sheets are tost away.
> He opes his snuff-box, hums an air,
> Then yawns and stretches in his chair.
> Not twenty, by the minute-hand!
> Good Gods, says he, my watch must stand!
> How muddling 'tis on books to pore!
> I thought I'd read an hour or more.
> The morning, of all hours, I hate.
> One can't contrive to rise too late.
> To make the minutes faster run,
> Then too his tiresome self to shun,
> To the next coffee-house he speeds,
> Takes up the news, some scraps he reads.
> Saunt'ring, from chair to chair he trails,
> Now drinks his tea, now bites his nails:
> He spies a partner of his woe;
> By chat afflictions lighter grow. . . .
> (11. 5-28)

This passage seems worth quoting at length because its sustaining of tone and its variety of invention are both significant accomplishments. Without falling to the temptation of making explicit judgments, Gay manages to convey perfectly the atmosphere and occupations of ennui. The techniques seem carefully calculated, beginning with the "What can *one* do?" (rather than "What can *I* do?"), with its implicit attempt on the part of the gentleman to universalize his plight—or perhaps, more accurately, its assumption that everyone else must be in essentially the same situation. The only occupation that really appeals to this victim of boredom is sleeping; to this idea alone he returns. The skillful use of the passive voice in relation to his "intellectual" activity (the attempt to read the pamphlet) stresses his lack of involvement: the pamphlet is spread before him (by a servant?); almost half a page is read, without volition on his part; equally without volition, the pages are tossed away. Then comes the inevitable rationalization: no lack of intellectual power on the reader's part produces his boredom; it is rather that the reading of books is a "muddling" activity. The alternatives he pursues might seem equally muddling, but at least they demand no involvement: one can open a snuffbox, hum, yawn, saunter from chair to chair in a coffee house, bite one's nails, drink one's tea, without thought or effort. Thus Gay conveys the damning verdict on his victim: this is man without reason, incapable of reason, his intellectual powers destroyed through his failure to use them—through, indeed, a peculiar variety of pride: pride in being a gentleman of leisure. The key line thematically is the weakest poetically: "Then too his tiresome self to shun." All life is tiresome to such a man, and it is a perfect circle of cause and effect: because he himself is tiresome, all activity seems tiresome to him; because all activity seems tiresome, he becomes ever more bored and boring. The passage presents a fine capsule portrait of a universal type seen so clearly as to seem almost an individual.

Perhaps the best way to perceive the special qualities of these fables is to compare some examples of the second group with their counterparts in the first series. Fable VII in the first series, "The Lyon, the Fox, and the Geese," deals with much the same subject matter as Fable II in the second series, "The Vultur, the Sparrow, and other Birds." Both explain an animal government and the way in which ministers are chosen and rule. The earlier one relates how a lion gives up the rule to a fox as viceroy. After everyone has bowed to the new regent, a fox steps forward to praise him as the model of prudence and mercy, concluding, "What blessings must attend the nation/ Under this good administration!" (ll. 27-28). A dissident goose, however, comments that " 'twas a fox who spoke th' oration" (l. 34), and observes that, when foxes praise a government "As gentle, plentiful and wise" (l. 36), geese are sure to suffer, for:

> ev'ry petty clerk in place,
> To prove his taste, and seem polite,
> Will feed on geese both noon and night.
> (ll. 40-42)

In the second fable, a greedy vulture gains the eagle monarch's ear and is named minister of state. He immediately replaces the nightingale with the daw as an official, surrounds the hawk with "Thousands of hireling Cocks" (1. 99), substitutes magpies for ravens. All this activity produces a statement from the sparrow:

> When rogues like these (a Sparrow cries)
> To honours and employments rise,
> I court no favour, ask no place;
> From such, preferment is disgrace:
> Within my thatch'd retreat I find
> (What these ne'er feel) true peace of mind.
> (11.109-14)

The difference in tone between the utterance of the goose in the early fable and that of the sparrow in the later one is apparent in even such short excerpts. Both birds speak out against the existing government, but their voices bear no resemblance to each other. The goose, frankly concerned with his own welfare, is nonetheless able to summon an ironic perspective, to perceive the universality of the situation and even its comic aspects. The pun on "taste" is a good example of the complicated tone. "Taste" here means, quite literally, "the physical sense of taste," as well as "the ability to discriminate"; the pun sums up the foxes' grossness in assuming that gluttony is, in effect, the test of culture. Moreover, the fact that the birds are geese implies a further joke on the author's part, a substratum of criticism for those who allow themselves to be taken over by corrupt governments. The fable is economical, emphatic; it demonstrates the nature of corruption instead of merely asserting it; it makes its point quickly and sharply, then abandons it.

The sparrow's attitude toward the evil he perceives is entirely different. Gay depicts this bird as he, the poet, sometimes depicts himself: smug, self-satisfied, secure in the consciousness that his position is the virtuous one. Nor does the author provide any further dimension of irony or perspective. The sparrow's voice is the only one here; none echoes behind it. Although what the bird says solidifies the moral statement of the poem, providing a clear alternative to the sort of pernicious involvement that other birds yield to, it does so in far too obvious a way. In the earlier fable, no image of virtue exists within the poem; such an image is assumed by the author to exist in his readers. The fact that Gay seems less secure about his readers in the later poem is one indication of its comparative weakness.

The later fable is not without strength, manifested in the seventy-four-line preamble, not the forty-line story which follows. Here is where Gay says directly, and sometimes even brilliantly, what he has to say. Two examples from this preliminary section have already been quoted, one as an indication of the power with which the poet can express directly his political passion; the other as an example of his weakness when speaking directly of himself. The power is, on the whole, more clearly manifested than the weakness. The opening lines, for example, with their ironic disclaimer of any intention to criticize specific social evils, is good Augustan satiric verse:

> E'er I begin, I must premise
> Our ministers are good and wise;
> So, though malicious tongues apply,
> Pray, what care they, or what care I?
> If I am free with courts; be't known,
> I ne'er presume to mean our own. . . .
> Our present schemes are too profound
> For *Machiavel* himself to sound:
> To censure 'em I've no pretension;
> I own they're past my comprehension.
> (11. 1-6, 13-16)

Once again Gay demonstrates his mastery of the colloquial tone; more importantly, he demonstrates his ability to use it to reinforce his self-image, for satiric purposes, as naïve, innocent, unsophisticated, removed from the concerns of the court ("what care I?"). Far more effective than direct statement about the author's virtue in setting up an image opposed to that of political corruption, this self-portrait, instead of claiming resistance to temptation, demonstrates complete removal from the realm of temptation. This opening establishes a convincing context for the telling of an animal tale: what could be more natural to the naïve poet who disclaims all responsibility for political effectiveness? And it is far more meaningful verse than that in the tale itself, which seems weak, contrived, and not really interesting *in itself* to the poet. What seems to engage him now is the message rather than the technique; one rarely finds the touches of brilliant characterization or direct perception that mark so many of the early fables. Such touches may still exist, but more often in long preambles than in the tales.

In the first series of fables, the theme of pride was both constant and profound; in the second series, it frequently seems comparatively superficial. Fable V, for example, "The Bear in a Boat," is dedicated "To a Coxcomb." Its preamble describes the nature of the coxcomb, who may be briefly defined, in Gay's terms, as a man destroyed by meaningless pride. Although it begins with the note of high seriousness and in the traditional language of eighteenth-century morality ("That man must daily wiser grow,/Whose search is bent himself to know" [11. 1-2]), it soon degenerates into examples so trivial that the theme is degraded. The specific instances of pride we are offered are the vanity of the man who fancies himself a lover, that of the man who crams his shelf with learning but fails to know himself, and that of the ambitious man who makes mistakes disastrous to the state because of self-esteem. The last is, of course, Walpole, and much of the preamble is a discussion of his specific vices. But—although these may be serious enough in relation to the conduct of government; although, indeed, the man who knows books but not himself is a genuine enough sinner—Gay seems quite to have lost consciousness of the metaphysical implications involved. That consciousness, which frequently dominates the first group of fables, is replaced in the second group by political awareness, with a resultant loss in complexity and power.

We can find things to praise in the second series of fables, but they are comparatively trivial. We may smile at the comic improbability of the comment of the ox in Fable XV on the subject of his own castration: "the barb'rous knife/Hath sever'd me from social life" (11. 85-86); or at such titles as "The Owl, the Swan, the Cock, the Spider, the Ass, and the Farmer" (Fable XIV). In neither case, however, can we be at all sure that the humor was intentional. We may admire an occasional precise concluding couplet: "By outward show let's not be cheated:/An ass should like an ass be treated" (Fable XI, 11. 99-100). But our very admiration may cause us to realize that such couplets are all too rare in the second series. The only talent really consistently employed in these tales is that of creating vignettes which define character convincingly and economically. The portrayal of the young nobleman trying to kill time is one good example; others are the description of the young heir in Fable XI and of the "modern politician" in Fable IX. This is a talent which forms the fables themselves in the first series; in the later group, it seems to manifest itself almost entirely in the preambles. Gay's interests appear to have shifted, his purposes to have changed. In the first series of fables he found ideal conditions for exercising his talents: a genre which permitted a valuable sort of aesthetic distance, which encouraged his ability to define sharply and quickly, which allowed for his sense of humor. In the second series he stretched the limits of the genre, with largely unfortunate results.

CHAPTER 5

The Poet's Plays

SHORTLY before *The Beggar's Opera* first opened, on January 29, 1728, Pope wrote to Swift: "John Gay's Opera is just on the point of Delivery. It may be call'd (considering its Subject) a Jayl-Delivery. Mr. Congreve . . . is anxious as to its Success, and so am I; whether it succeeds or not, it will make a great noise, but whether of Claps or Hisses I know not. At worst it is in its own nature a thing which he can *lose* no reputation by, as he lays none upon it." [1] (Gay's Latin motto for the play, from Martial, was "*Nos haec novimus esse nihil*," "We know this to be nothing.") *The Beggar's Opera* was, however, from its first performance an enormous—indeed, an unparalleled—success. Gay wrote to Swift on February 15 that it had been performed fifteen times "and 'tis thought it will run a fortnight longer." [2] It was actually to be offered an unprecedented sixty-two times during the first season, closing on June 19.[3]

Yet despite the play's enormous popularity (portraits of its principal actors were sold throughout London, appearing even on fans and screens; a set of playing cards bore its songs; Lavinia Fenton, the actress whose reputation was made by her playing of Polly, had to be escorted home at night by guards lest the crowds make off with her), controversy attended it from its earliest days. The principal issue was moral: must not a play whose hero was a highwayman, all of whose characters came from the criminal classes, contribute by this very fact to public immorality; would it not encourage young men to imitate Macheath? The Reverend Thomas Herring, later to become Archbishop of York and of Canterbury, preached against the opera "as a Thing of every evil Tendency." [4] Newspapers and journals recorded the arrests of men disastrously influenced by Macheath and his friends: a stroller named Hutchinson was committed to jail as a forger, seized as he was about to act the part of Captain Macheath; antagonistic commentators recorded many similar instances of corruption supposedly caused directly or indirectly by the play.

Later that year a whole book appeared on the theme: *Thievery A-la-mode: or The Fatal Encouragement.* It recounts the history of a young man, vainly trying to seek his fortune, who witnesses *The Beggar's Opera* and later observes everywhere the portraits of Macheath and Polly on fans, snuff boxes, and the like. Discovering that these characters are universally admired, the unfortunate young man becomes himself a highwayman, remarking to a victim, "This, Sir, . . . is but the Sequel of the *Beggar's Opera;* and I hope no Gentleman will be offended at the *Reality,* who was delighted with the *Representation.*" [5] Finally, predictably, he comes to his deathbed as a result of his evil ways, and confesses his misdeeds, "concluding with a hearty Prayer, that he might be the only person seduced by the extravagant Applause the Town gave the Character of a Thief in the *Beggar's Opera.*" [6] It is irrelevant to our immediate concerns, but perhaps suggestive of the nature of eighteenth-century popular morality, to note that at this juncture his sister arrives with news of an inheritance adequate to both their needs, and the hero dies regretting that he had not postponed his life of crime since it would not have been necessary if he had waited.

Attacks on the morality of *The Beggar's Opera* continued throughout the century—and so, of course, did frequent representations. In 1729 a poem purported to "dissect" *The Beggar's Opera,* with the preliminary ground of attack that a taste for such plays implied corresponding scorn for the great tragedies of the past: "Rouze then ye *Briton's!* Rouse at *Shakespear's* Call,/His Hamlet suffers by this spurious Droll." [7] The poem indicts the opera for moral dubiousness:

> with uncommon Art,
> The Old are harden'd, and the Young are taught,
> To act those Vices, which too soon will smart.
> (8)

Later in the century, attacks were more far-reaching, if even less poetically skillful:

> An easy elegance in *Gay* we trace
> But not one sentiment replete with grace;
> His op'ra certainly is very smart,
> But not one sentence there can touch the heart;
> Besides, to immorality it tends,
> And vice, with colours much too pleasing blends. . . .
> To set forth vice, too pleasingly exprest,
> Tempts us to copy, what we should detest.
> Many, through seeing gay Macheath, have glow'd,
> To rise the foremost champions of the road;
> Panted for lawrel's of heroic shame;
> Wounded their conscience, and destroy'd their fame;
> And Oh! I wish this captivating pest,
> In prudence, by the managers suppress.[8]

Sir John Fielding in 1772 appealed to David Garrick to stop subsequent performances of *The Beggar's Opera,* since, he claimed, it was never shown without creating more thieves. The *Gentleman's Magazine,* reporting this, added: "The Beggars Opera is, in truth, the thief's creed and common-prayer book, in which he fortifies himself in the most atrocious wickedness, from the impunity and triumph of his great exampler Macheath; and comforts himself, that, notwithstanding he may be hanged for his robbery, he is no worse than his betters." [9] Like some commentators on Gay's *Fables,* the outraged moralist who offers this judgment seems to suspect that he has been somehow betrayed.

By 1777 the reaction against the comedy was more intense. Sir John Hawkins wrote that it had "been productive of more mischief to this country than any would believe" at the time of its first representation, principally because "the tendency of it, by inculcating that persons in authority are actuated by the same motives as thieves and robbers is, to destroy all confidence in ministers, and respect for magistrates." [10] A new acted version of the play, produced during the same year, sums up clearly the nature of moralistic objections to it. A magazine account of the adaptation, presented with singular tonal ambiguity, is at least perfectly clear about the essential viciousness of Gay's play: "That the Beggar's Opera has long had a vicious effect on the minds of the ignorant, is a fact ascertainable by a volume of evidence easily collected from the . . . Newgate Calendars." Then comes a précis of the new version: the Beggar and the Player now have a colloquy, toward the end of the original text, in which the Beggar announces that he wishes to make his drama moral. Consequently, Macheath's sentence is remitted to three years of hard labor as a ballast heaver. Several remarks on the beauty of a virtuous life follow this decision; then Macheath is shown heaving ballast and acknowledging the justice of his fate. "This alteration," comments the magazine, "our readers will perceive, is extremely moral, they must not, therefore, wonder, if they find it somewhat dull in representation. Morality and dullness are frequently stage companions." Yet the ends of poetical justice are indeed served by the change, the account continues—and the audience can always leave before the end.[11] One wonders whether the audience took the changes as lightly as the magazine writer seems to.

Of course *The Beggar's Opera* had its ardent defenders from the beginning. The most distinguished of these was Gay's friend Swift, who devoted a number of *The Intelligencer* to "A Vindication of Mr. Gay, and the Beggars Opera." Swift attacked directly the problem of morality, insisting that the truth was the reverse of general opinion: far from increasing immorality, the play could only improve standards. "In this happy Performance of Mr. *Gay's*," he writes, "all the Characters are just, and none of them carried beyond Nature, or hardly beyond Practice. It discovers the whole System of the Common-Wealth, or that *Imperium in Impervio* of Iniquity, established among us, by which neither our Lives, nor our Properties are secure, either in the High-ways, or in public Assemblies, or even in our own Houses. . . ."[12] He concludes forcefully: "Upon the Whole, I deliver my Judgment, That nothing but servile Attachment to a Party, Affectation of Singularity, lamentable Dullness, mistaken Zeal, or studied Hypocrisy, can have the least reasonable Objection against this excellent moral Performance."[13]

The opera had other defenders at least as emphatic in insisting that Gay's piece served the ends of morality. Gibbon, to be sure, was to suggest "that the production of *The Beggar's Opera* brought about a refinement in the manners of actual thieves, 'making them less ferocious, more polite, in fact, more like gentlemen'"[14]—a curious notion about a play whose satiric purpose was rather to make gentlemen themselves less like thieves! An anonymous poem entitled *The Modern Poet. A Rapsody,* far from assuming the characters to be models of vice, takes them rather as exemplars of virtue:

> Dukes, Earls, and Knights, to *Lincoln's* Theatre throng,
> To hear themselves lash'd in each painted Song. . . .
> The Ladies blush at their unguarded Folly,
> To see the Virtue, that they want, in *Polly.*[15]

The poet goes on to attack Italian opera, making a comparison, much to the advantage of Gay, between it and *The Beggar's Opera:* Italian opera is comparatively superficial, a genre for which "pompous Scenes, at great Expence, are bought,/Whilst *Gay's,* alas! can only boast of Thought."[16]

This comment reminds us of another reason for the enormous popularity of Gay's play in the eighteenth century. Many contemporary phenomena contributed to the astounding enthusiasm with which it was received; one of these was the early eighteenth-century popularity of Italian opera, a form which Gay's ballad opera was thought to attack. The Beggar's early comments point explicitly to the play's relation to opera: "I have introduc'd the Similes that are in all your celebrated *Operas:* The *Swallow,* the *Moth,* the *Bee,* the *Ship,* the *Flower,* &c. Besides I have a Prison Scene, which the Ladies always reckon charmingly pathetick. . . . I hope I may be forgiven, that I have not made my Opera throughout unnatural, like those in vogue; for I have no Recitative: Excepting this, as I have consented to have neither Prologue nor Epilogue, it must be allow'd an Opera in all its forms."[17] Swift assumed that the comedy was intended to expose "that unnatural Taste for *Italian* Musick among us, which is wholly unsuitable to our Northern *Climate,* and the *Genius* of the People, whereby we are overrun with *Italian-Effeminacy,* and *Italian* Nonsense. An old Gentleman said to me, that many Years ago, when the Practice of an unnatural Vice grew so frequent in *London* that many were prosecuted for it, he was sure it would be the Fore-runner of *Italian Opera's* and Singers; and then we should want nothing but stabbing or poysoning, to make us perfect Italians."[18]

Yet, although contemporary audiences were titillated by the

jokes they detected in Gay's play about Italian opera in general and even perhaps about specific examples of it, it is by no means certain that Gay had in mind more than a glancing attack on opera. As Bertrand H. Bronson puts it, after a thorough and convincing exploration of the relation between *The Beggar's Opera* and contemporary examples of grand opera,[19] "There is little probability that Gay intended a serious attack upon Italian opera, and he may even have been somewhat appalled at the amount of damage caused by his play. For his ridicule does not go beyond poking affectionate fun at conventions which, like most conventions objectively regarded, have their ludicrous side."[20] And again: "Everything considered, *The Beggar's Opera* may more properly be regarded as a testimonial to the strength of opera's appeal to John Gay's imagination than as a deliberate attempt to ridicule it out of existence."[21]

A second reason for the comedy's great audience appeal was its readily apparent satire on Walpole and his cohorts. Gay's distaste for the prime minister, recorded also, as we have seen, in the *Fables,* was an important theme of his play; if Walpole himself refused to acknowledge the fact, applauding gallantly on opening night, no one else was in much doubt about it. Walpole was notorious for taking bribes, for other elaborate financial manipulations, and also for womanizing. Both aspects of his character are considered in the play; the audience's attention is drawn to the comedy's satiric relevance by Peachum's list of aliases for Walpole, applied to a member of Peachum's gang: "*Robin* of *Bagshot,* alias *Gorgon,* alias *Bluff Bob,* alias *Carbuncle,* alias *Bob Booty*" (I, 140).

Audiences could enjoy the not at all vicious satire in the play (as Irving puts it, "No reforming zest is there"[22]) and vie to find new examples of it; they could respond to the excitement of an unusual group of characters (made yet more striking, on occasion, by the presence of men in the women's parts and vice versa; this was a favorite entertainment of the eighteenth century, and the *Gentleman's Magazine* for April, 1782, contains the death notice of one Mrs. Fitzherbert, who died of hysterics, having begun to laugh uncontrollably at seeing Polly represented by a man); they could enjoy the lilting music, which included many old country tunes made suddenly respectable by their new context. Perhaps partly because the play's excellence is extremely difficult to define, early discussions center mainly on its essentially extra-literary merits. But in the twentieth century, when only specialists are likely to be interested in attacks on Walpole or on Italian opera, when the titillation of viewing "low" characters on stage has long since vanished in a flood of such characters, when country tunes are quite respectable in their own right—in the twentieth century we need to define different reasons for our continued enjoyment. The specifically literary problems *The Beggar's Opera* presents are both absorbing and complex.

Considering what we have discovered about Gay's poetry thus far, we should not find it surprising that his most spectacular success and his most enduring fame resulted from a play: the dramatic form itself helps to solve the artistic problem that persistently plagued Gay. A stage representation by its nature provides a marked distance between author and character, supplies automatic perspective; the sort of confusion Gay manifests in, say, *The Shepherd's Week,* is not apparent in *The Beggar's Opera* and the plays which preceded and followed it. Yet the ambiguities suggested by the curious shifts of tone in the poetry persist in the plays and find expression both in the weakest and in the strongest of Gay's dramatic efforts. The dispute over the morality of *The Beggar's Opera* can be seen as a demonstration of this fact: the central question concerns the nature of the audience's feelings toward the characters, which are presumably at least partially controlled by the author's feelings.

The way Gay expected his audiences to feel toward Macheath and Polly is by no means perfectly clear. The two most provocative modern essays on *The Beggar's Opera,* those by William Empson and Professor Bronson, both discuss this complicated point at length. "Indeed," remarks Empson, "the fascination of this character [Polly] is that one has no means of telling whether she is simple or ironical." [23] He examines at length the various ambiguities of Polly's character; everyone else in the play is almost equally susceptible to similar examination. Professor Bronson isolates the opera's various levels of satire, which depend largely upon one's varying interpretation of the characters. "Each of the leading characters," he observes, "is a positive force." [24] But he then demonstrates that "with the possible exception of Polly, they all have a better opinion of themselves than we do,"[25] that the satire which focuses beyond the characters, on their betters, and farther still, on twentieth-century audiences themselves, depends upon one's shifting sense of the value judgments to be attached to the personages of the play. In *The Beggar's Opera* the ambiguities are valuable; they are not useful in the earlier plays (in which divisions of sympathy work against rather than for maximum effectiveness). These early plays comprise a sequence of experimentation for which *The Beggar's Opera* provides the logical culmination.

II

Even Gay's first play, *The Mohocks* (1712), shows complicated waverings in point of view. Described by Gay as "a tragi-comical farce," it is actually pure farce, with characters conceived as puppet images. Yet the play has some relation to contemporary actuality: the Mohocks were bands of upper-class young men who terrorized London early in 1712, committing various outrages upon innocent pedestrians who encountered them. Gay's treatment of them is characteristically ambiguous in tone.

A key literary device of *The Mohocks,* which has been fully documented by T. B. Stroup,[26] is its reliance on Miltonic imitation. When, at the opening of the play, the villainous Mohocks discuss their activities, they do so in the precise mode of Milton's devils:

> Thus far our riots with success are crown'd,
> Have found no stop, or what they found o'ercame;
> In vain th' embattel'd Watch in deep array,
> Against our rage oppose their lifted poles;
> Through Poles we rush triumphant, watchman rolls
> On watchman; while their lanthorns kick'd aloft
> Like blazing stars, illumine all the air.
>
> (*Plays* I, 7)

They enroll a new recruit; the Emperor of the Mohocks orders them to "search with care th' intentions of his heart,/See he be not a superficial sinner" (8). When the candidate survives investigation, he is duly enrolled under the name of "Cannibal" ("like them, devour mankind," commands the Emperor). Then the gang swears together a mighty oath:

> That we'll to virtue bear invet'rate hate,
> Renounce humanity, defy religion;
> That villany, and all outrageous crimes
> Shall ever be our glory and our pleasure.
> (I, 9)

Why does Gay wish thus to connect the Mohocks with the genuinely diabolical, giving them some of the poetic dignity of Milton's devils? Is he, like Milton, a true poet and of the devil's party without knowing it; or is his purpose simply to burlesque? Certainly the early image of the watchmen's lanterns illumining the air like blazing stars, like that of watchman rolling upon watchman, is simply ludicrous. Yet the Miltonic imitation is more than a joke, for it hints that behind the libertinage of the Mohocks lies a set of principles, however reprehensible; that criminal defiance of society can be conscious and meaningful.

The members of the watch opposed in the play to the Mohocks lack any equivalent suggestions of dignity. Instead of blank verse, they speak in a prose that has frequent affinities with that of such "low" Shakespearian characters as Dogberry. The watchmen are cowards, comic liars ("I saw them cut off a fellow's legs, and if the poor man had not run hard for it, they cut off his head into the bargain" [I, 12]), and hypocrites, who pretend always to be braver than they are. They have the charm of their common humanity but they offer nothing to admire. The action of the play stresses their ludicrous incompetence. Forced to exchange clothes and roles with the criminals, they lack the courage to reveal or to defy their tormentors. The wife of one of them finally unmasks the villains; then, given superiority of numbers ("it shall all out—faith—now I have got all my friends about me" [I, 25]) and the obvious discomfiture of the Mohocks, the watchmen become brave enough to tell the truth.

As in most farces, there is no clear center of sympathy in the play, but neither is there any definite focus of mockery. The Mohocks are more dignified than their victims, but they degenerate into sniveling at the end ("We'll submit, ask pardon, or do anything" [I, 26]). Those who suffer at their hands seem natural buffoons and butts, born to be victims; this is as true of the elegant gentleman they waylay as of the constabulary. The play suggests, through its farcical tone, its author's conviction that the general disturbance over the depredations of the Mohocks is itself a laughing matter: beyond this, nothing is clear. The representatives of law and order are more ridiculous than the criminals; the criminals occasionally approach a moral grandeur quite foreign to their adversaries, yet they define themselves by their activities as clearly despicable. What, finally, are members of an audience to think? What, exactly, are they being invited to laugh at?

Actually, *The Mohocks* never found an audience; no producer would offer it, and Gay printed it without having it acted. *The Wife of Bath,* his next dramatic attempt, met a slightly better fate: it was acted at Drury Lane on May 12, 1713, and for two nights thereafter, before being withdrawn. If *The Mohocks* suggests, in its peculiar attitudes toward law and criminality, some of the complexities of feeling that were to make *The Beggar's Opera* perplexing, *The Wife of Bath* offers reflections on marriage, femininity, and pedigree that also presage the later play. "Matrimony throws one at once off from the Conversation of the *Beau Monde*" observes Doggrell—"a Husband among them is neither allow'd to be handsome, well bred, or witty.—he loses all his former *Politesse* with his Liberty." [27] The world and its language revealed here bear strong similarities to those of the later play. But, whereas Macheath's comments on *politesse* issue from a clearly conceived character with a forceful and consistent point of view, the natural product of his personality, in Doggrell's remarks the wit is clearly the author's, not the character's. Although Doggrell is consistent in his distaste for marriage and in his high regard for his own family and his own poetry, he is never more than a mouthpiece. All the play's characters seem roles rather than personalities.

The structure of the plot suggests Gay's characteristic division of sympathy. As W. H. Irving puts it, it is a "broken-backed plot. The interest is continually divided between the Florinda-Merit and the Myrtilla-Chaucer episodes." [28] Moreover, the tone shifts erratically from bawdy farce to sentimental romance. More than ever, the playwright appears unable to commit himself fully. He can temporarily advocate some idea with apparent conviction—there is great clarity, for example, in this interchange:

Merit: In short, Sir,—she is a plain, simple *Kentish* Yeoman's Daughter—she has Virtue without Formality—all the good Breeding of the Court with the Country Simplicity—Beauty without Vanity, and Wit without Affectation.

Doggrell: But a Family, Sir, would add a Lustre to these Endowments; and these Qualities appear very awkward in a Woman of mean Extraction.

Merit: Virtue, Sir, becomes all alike, and there's no true Nobility without it. (3)

But without the ironic tensions of *The Beggar's Opera* to qualify the simplicity of Merit's unexceptionable moralizing such sequences are merely dull. Weak in action, characterization, and language, *The Wife of Bath* seems the work of a man with only superficial interest in his material.

III

Gay followed the failure of *The Wife of Bath* with the relative success of *The What d'ye Call It* (1715), acted twenty-eight times the first two seasons, revived frequently until 1750, and issued in six editions during the author's lifetime; it earned him a hundred pounds. The play, permeated with literary satire, appears to have been an offshoot of Gay's association with the Scriblerus Club. Even by modern standards, *The What d'ye Call It*—far more interesting in itself and in Gay's development, than either of its predecessors—deserved its mild success. Its form, if form it can be called ("tragi-comi-pastoral farce"), appears to have fascinated Gay, who discusses it at length in his preface—not, of course, with perfect seriousness. The real justification for the mixture of genres comes from Sir Roger in the first scene: "And is the play as I ordered it, both a Tragedy and a Comedy? I would have it a pastoral too; and if you could make it a farce, so much the better—and what if you croun'd all with the spice of your Opera? You know my neighbours never saw a play before; and d'ye see, I would shew them all sorts of plays under one" (I, 39). The implicit disrespect of the playwright for his audience is clear throughout the play.

But the apparent lack of seriousness in the play's structure disguises, in this case, serious ideas. *The What d'ye Call It* reveals a good deal about the young Gay, through the same sorts of ambiguities and concealments that are characteristic of

The Shepherd's Week and even parts of *Trivia*. This speech by the aunt is representative:

> O tyrant Justices! have you forgot
> How my poor brother was in *Flanders* shot?
> You pres'd my brother—he shall walk in white,
> He shall—and shake your curtains ev'ry night.
> What though the paultry hare he rashly kill'd,
> That cross'd the furrows while he plough'd the field?
> You sent him o'er the hills and far away;
> Left his old mother to the parish pay,
> With whom he shared his ten-pence ev'ry day.

She then supplies a list of other poor folk who have been ruined by the law for minor offenses, concluding,

> Now will you press my harmless nephew too?
> Ah, what has conscience with the rich to do!
> (I, 43)

The aunt is clearly right in her condemnation of the rich; the entire action of the play supports her. The play within a play centers on the plight of the poor countryman unjustly impressed into the army because a girl complains that he has seduced her. The denouement, however, reveals that the actual seducer was the squire's son, who gave his victim two gold guineas to lie about the identity of her betrayer. Another country soldier, who has been similarly drafted, is to be executed for his lack of bloodthirstiness; he could be saved by a bribe to the corporal. The three justices who preside over the proceedings are attacked by a chorus of ghosts (including, notably, the ghost of an embryo!); each spirit is that of someone whose death the justices have caused. And, in the enveloping action, not only do the justices turn out to be fools (in character much like the "hero" of "The Birth of the Squire"), but the squire's son is unmasked as a real-life seducer. All the problems are happily resolved—this is, after all, comedy and farce, hardly at all "tragedy"—but the nature of the problems emphasizes the central fact that the rich and powerful are morally inferior to the poor and virtuous, that the supposition of vice can attach almost automatically to anyone in authority.

Yet this point of view is qualified in this play much as it is in

The Shepherd's Week—which, in tone, language, and situation, the play frequently closely resembles. The aunt's speech is a good example of the way in which Gay uses his characters' language to comment upon their sentiments. The incongruity between the aunt's claim of injustice and her invocation of revenge in the form of a curtain-shaking ghost makes it impossible for us to sympathize fully with the character; she (like all her fellows) is deliberately made farcical although her claims are both serious and valid. Her final cry ("Ah, what has conscience with the rich to do!") comes clearly from the heart. The pathos of the disproportion between the triviality of her brother's crime and the magnitude of its punishment is obscured by her attempts at grand language ("What though the paultry hare he rashly kill'd"). Once again, Gay by the very nature of his form protects himself from the appearance of involvement. In the preface he makes a straightforward statement of his attitude toward country folk: "To the . . . objection which is the meanness of the sentiments, I answer, that the sentiments of Princes and clouns have not in reality that difference which they seem to have: their thoughts are almost the same, and they only differ as the same thought is attended with a meanness or pomp of diction, or receive a different light from the circumstances each Character is conversant with" (I, 32). The germ of *The Beggar's Opera* is here: the perception that the rich and the poor are essentially alike makes potential a full satire of a class-dominated society. In this early play, however, Gay did not really follow the hint he himself offered. The *dissimilarity* of rich and poor is constantly emphasized, to the moral, if not the stylistic, advantage of the poor. The satirist's material is clearly there; the satirist's perception appears in the preface; but material and perception are not unified although, more clearly than either of its predecessors, this play offers a promise for the future.

IV

For clearly focused satire we must wait for *Three Hours After Marriage* (1717), in which Gay was helped to an indeterminate extent by Pope and Arbuthnot. The extent of the collaboration remains unclear. Certainly the play is far more sophisticated than any preceding dramatic work of Gay's, and its models in Restoration comedy are not those we would expect him to employ. On the other hand, Pope refers to it several times as "Gay's play," and Gay himself, after the riotous reception of the play, accepts responsibility for it in a letter to Pope:

Too late I see, and confess myself mistaken, in Relation to the Comedy, yet I do not think had I follow'd your Advice, and only introduc'd the *Mummy*, that the Absence of the Crocodile had sav'd it. I can't help laughing myself, (though the Vulgar do not consider that it was design'd to look very ridiculous) to think how the poor Monster and Mummy were dash'd at their Reception, and when the Cry was loudest, thought that if the Thing had been wrote by another, I should have deem'd the Town in some Measure mistaken, and as to your Apprehension that this may do us future Injury, do not think it; the Doctor has a more valuable Name than can be hurt by any Thing of this Nature, and yours is doubly safe; I will (if any Shame there be) take it all to myself, as indeed I ought, the Motion being first mine, and never heartily approv'd of by you.[29]

(The mummy and crocodile were particularly bizarre touches in the rather bawdy play: two would-be lovers, determined to cuckold a new husband, choose these disguises as a mode of introducing themselves into his house. The early riots at the play's production included "hoots of derison" at "each fresh absurdity" of this sort.[30]) Irving states unequivocally, "It is reasonably clear that the original idea and all the structural organization of the play were Gay's."[31]

Lacking specific knowledge about *which* details of action and language were Gay's we can base little interpretation of his dramatic career on this particular instance of comic invention. The play is very funny indeed: a recent editor has described it as "one of the wittiest plays in the language and one of the most neglected."[32] Its verbal humor does not seem quite in Gay's early mode; in structure, on the other hand, it repeats certain devices that were beginning to seem characteristic of his dramatic technique. Disguise is a central dramatic device of *The Mohocks;* it precipitates marriage for some characters and sexual gratification for others in *The Wife of Bath;* in a more complicated form, it makes possible the marriage in *The What d'ye Call It.* In *Three Hours After Marriage* disguises come thick and fast; the entire play is a farce of pretenses. If none of the disguises really accomplish much, they yet remain the center of the action—and the point of the action, in a sense, is that nothing much is accomplished. Through Gay's later plays, too, this theme was to run, becoming increasingly dominant. In *The Beggar's Opera* it was to take, as we shall see, its most complicated form.

Frequently the mode of disguise is related to, or depends upon, some form of dramatic representation *within* the play. *The What d'ye Call It* is, of course, framed by this notion of drama within drama; a framework encloses *The Beggar's Opera* and *The Rehearsal at Goatham,* the last of Gay's plays to be published, has a play as subject. And in *Three Hours After Marriage* one of the most important comic characters, Phoebe Clinket, is an aspiring playwright, deluded by her interest in drama into total unawareness of reality, and capable of producing one of the play's final jokes by bragging of her "fertility": in the production of plays, not children.

Better symbols than those of disguise could hardly be found for Gay's own difficulties as a writer in focusing on one point of view toward a given character or experience. His sense of life's ambiguities is repeatedly recorded and re-emphasized, as he shows his characters constantly making their identities deliberately dubious. Are Plotwell and Underplot less or more themselves in the casing of mummy and crocodile? When the character Chaucer disguises himself as an astrologer and fortuneteller and predicts the future of the girl he loves, does he not thus dramatize his comic verve and love of excitement more tellingly than he could in his normal guise? Perhaps the most revealing instance of all is the "disguise" of the squire's son in *The What d'ye Call It.* In the guise of a countryman he can escape for the first time the corrupt values of his class; it becomes possible—as it was not before—for him to marry the girl he has wronged when he plays the role of country bumpkin in the farcical play-within-the-play.

None of these episodes, of course, will really bear the weight of extended analysis, for all exist in farcical contects which remove significance from them. Yet they point to Gay's preoccupation with the problem of reality as it relates to the true nature of human beings. The difficulty of perceiving truth about people, of isolating truth about character from truth about social level and its implications: this is the subject that seems to have preoccupied Gay in both his plays and his poetry.

V

Gay's dramatic efforts had hitherto been only in comedy. In 1720 however, he attempted a new mode: pastoral tragedy. His sense of daring in the venture is suggested by his prologue to that play, *Dione:*

> Yet still methinks our author's fate I dread.
> Were it not safer beaten paths to tread
> Of Tragedy; than o'er wide heaths to stray,
> And seeking strange adventures lose his way? . . .
> there's danger in't, 'tis true;
> Yet spare him, as he gives you something new.
> (11. 29-31, 39-40)

Never acted, this excursion into pastoral attracted little attention. Dr. Johnson condemned it: "A Pastoral of an hundred lines may be endured; but who will hear of sheep and goats, and myrtle bowers and purling rivulets, through five acts? Such scenes please Barbarians in the dawn of literature, and children in the dawn of life; but will be for the most part thrown away as men grow wise, and nations grow learned." [33]

The difficulty *Dione* presents to modern readers seems not so much a matter of too many sheep and goats as of Gay's familiar unsureness of purpose. The play (which, incidentally, relies heavily on the disguise motif) contains passages of great delicacy and charm; it makes serious and frequently beautiful use of the animal imagery (with particular emphasis on birds) which was later to dominate, with ironic intent, *The Beggar's Opera.* But it intersperses its pastoral beauties with singularly unconvincing and inappropriate satire of city and court life. Although every example in the play of rural love is desperately ill-fated, *Dione* sings the praises of rural happiness in love; the satiric sections seem equally unrooted in reality. The artificiality of the plot is not finally justified by its charm, and one agrees with Dr. Johnson: the play is meaninglessly long.

Little more can be said for Gay's next attempt at tragedy, this time in a more conventional vein. *The Captives* (first produced on January 15, 1724) is a bombastic heroic tragedy from the pen responsible for the satire of tragic bombast in *The What d'ye Call It* and in *Three Hours After Marriage*. Although it was both a popular and a financial success, it is by modern standards appalling, its characters implausible, its action emptily contrived, its verse crude:

> Think not to hide what is already known.
> 'Tis to *Sophernes* that you owe those chains:
> We've fathomed his designs, they're all laid open;
> We know him turbulent and enterprizing. . . .
> (*Plays* I, 93)

Verse of this quality dominates the play: Gay may have been conscious of its feebleness, for he never again attempted tragedy.

Indeed, his next dramatic effort was as different as possible from *The Captives*. In 1728 *The Beggar's Opera* appeared, to be followed the next year by its sequel, *Polly*. We may postpone detailed consideration of these crucially important works until we have taken a look at Gay's final plays: *Acis and Galatea*, the short pastoral opera Gay wrote with Handel some ten years before its first production in 1732; and three comedies, all published posthumously, the last of them never produced: *Achilles, The Distress'd Wife,* and *The Rehearsal at Goatham*. *Acis and Galatea* can hardly be considered a literary work. In isolation from its music, like most libretti, it is weak in plot and language. Some of its delicacy and charm survive, but it does not invite close examination.

Achilles has more obvious literary appeal. Its form is essentially that of *The Beggar's Opera:* prose dialogue interspersed with ballads; its content has great comic possibilities, by no means fully realized in Gay's treatment. The action centers on the situation when Achilles, at his mother's insistence, is disguised as a woman in order to avoid involvement in the Trojan War. In the first page or so it seems that Gay is going to write a play which, like *The Beggar's Opera*, exploits the ironic incongruity of making characters whom we think of as belonging to quite another sphere talk in the refined and empty language of eighteenth-century society. Thus Achilles, pleading with his mother not to disgrace him, observes "On the first step of a young fellow, depends his character for life.—I beg you, goddess, to dispense with your commands." And Thetis replies: "Have you then no regard to my presentiment? I can't bear the thoughts of your going; for I know that odious siege of *Troy* wou'd be the death of thee" (II, 159). The contraction ("can't") and the fashionable "odious" prepare us perfectly for the final locution, "wou'd be the death of thee," which removes all seriousness from the matter and turns a mother's fears for her son's life into the fashionable posturings of a woman of quality.

But after the opening pages the language no longer seems so carefully controlled, and Gay explores only the most obvious comic possibilities. There is the predictable bawdy joking: the king attempts to seduce Achilles in his woman's disguise, two men fight a duel over his favors, he seduces the princess with whom he shares a bedroom and makes her pregnant. The disguise theme, at the outset, provides the opportunity for some telling observations on the similarities between men and women. Thetis delivers them, as she wonders about the possible success of her son's disguise:

> Yet, after all, why *shou'd* I fear a discovery? for women have the same passions, though they employ 'em upon different objects. . . . He [Achilles] is sudden, he is impatient. What then? Are women less so? Ask almost all servants what they know of their mistresses.—He is wilful, testy, and untractable. Can't thousands of husbands say as much of their wives? Then as for his obstinacy—that never can shew him less a woman. But he hath not that command of his tongue I cou'd wish him: He is too vehement, too severe in his expressions. In this particular, indeed, few women take equal liberties to one another's faces, but they make ample amends for it behind each other's backs; so that, with all these infirmities of man, he may with the least conduct very well pass for a fine spirited woman.
>
> (II, 164–65)

This is not only a good joke, in context, it is also a significant one, underlining the importance of the disguise motif. For the first time, the point suggested by Gay's earlier uses of disguise in drama becomes explicit: that disguise can be—and frequently is—a means of revealing rather than concealing truth. The truth that men and women are alike in their weaknesses of character is fairly revolutionary in a time when comic drama depended so heavily on conventions about their differences, and we might wish that Gay had investigated it more thoroughly.

But the chief literary characteristic of *Achilles* is desultoriness. As the play continues, Gay relies more and more on repeating the techniques—and, he must have hoped, the success—of *The Beggar's Opera.* One of the tunes comes directly from the earlier play; several songs are rehashes of earlier themes and metaphors, far less appropriate in this new context. Thus a song by Theaspe, the queen, might more fittingly come from Mrs. Peachum:

> All hearts are a little frail
> When temptation is rightly apply'd.
> What can shame or fear avail
> When we sooth both ambition and pride?
> All women have power in view;
> Then there's pleasure to tempt her too.
> Such a sure attack there's no defying,
> No denying;
> Since complying
> Gives her another's due.
>
> (II, 175)

The sentiments seem, in Theaspe's mouth, far more mechanical than they do in Mrs. Peachum's. Her reactions to her husband's putative unfaithfulness follow a fixed and predictable pattern, producing none of the rich surprises of *The Beggar's Opera.* When Achilles sings:

> Shou'd the beast of the noblest race
> Act the brute of the lowest class;
> Tell me, which do you think more base,
> Or the lion or the ass?
>
> (II, 177)

—sings this to a pimping court officer, the imagery seems obvious and, lacking the emphatic reiteration which animal imagery receives in *The Beggar's Opera,* quite automatic and unconvincing. The rich comic *idea* of *Achilles* is weakened by the play's hackwork execution.

VI

The progression—or retrogression—of Gay's plays resembles that of his poetry. One becomes sharply aware of this fact reading *The Distress'd Wife,* first acted in 1734, a little more than a year after Gay's death, but not printed until 1743. Its relation to *The Beggar's Opera* is strikingly similar to the relation of the second series of *Fables* (also published posthumously) to the first. The strength of the first *Fables,* like that of *The Beggar's Opera,* lay largely in their complexity and ambiguity; the second series clarified, simplified, and weakened the point of view. One of the concerns of *The Beggar's Opera,* as William Empson has demonstrated, was the relative merits of the bourgeois and the aristocratic scheme of values. The play criticizes both sides, it does not permit any single ideological position.

By the time he wrote *The Distress'd Wife,* however, Gay had apparently made his choice. "We live on in the humdrum way of honesty and regularity," remarks the merchant Barter to Lady Willit: "We think, we act differently from people at your end of the town; and as it never yet was known, can it now be expected, that courtiers should ever stoop to regulate their conduct by ours?" (II, 218). Or again, without even the attempt at socially acceptable irony: "What is it that supports every individual of our country?—'Tis commerce.—On what depends the glory, the credit, the power of the Nation?—On commerce.— To what does the crown itself owe its splendour and dignity?— To commerce—to what owe you the revenues of your own half-ruin'd estates? To commerce: and are you so ungrateful then to treat the profession with contempt by which you are maintain'd? . . . When people of rank and figure can profess gaming, I am not surpriz'd that we are so contemptible; for commerce is the very reverse of it.—In gaming, one man's gain is t'other's ruin; but commerce is for the mutual advantage of both" (II, 259-60).

Here is a perfectly open statement of a naïve (surely the notion that commerce, unlike gambling, never ruins one man for the sake of another will hardly bear examination—in his poems Gay demonstrates awareness of the converse) but emphatic position to which Gay apparently gave full assent. Nothing in the play undercuts the integrity and essential nobility of Mr. Barter; the other admirable figure is a pathetic poor relation, Friendless (although it is interesting to note that the reward for her virtue is the privilege of marrying a lord!). The nobility is mocked and exposed as corrupt. The best that can be said for the aristocracy is that one of its members, Sir Thomas, under the guidance and surveillance of Barter, attempts to mend his ways.

This simple moral vision emerges through a plot heavily indebted to Restoration comedy, although with most of the spice removed. In this eighteenth-century version no one really has love affairs (except, to be sure, a servant girl, corrupted by an aristocrat), but everyone talks about imaginary liaisons: appearance is accepted as equivalent to actuality. Lady Willit herself observes this fact: "Half of the women in town have had nothing but the vanity of having lost their reputation.—Sure there was a time when men and women had other pleasures besides vanity!—The flirting fellows now play at making love, as the children make believe gossipings and christenings" (II, 228).

Reality exists only in the firm values of Barter and his like, and in the country; the conflict between aristocracy and bourgeoisie is reflected by that between city and country. Sir Thomas's reformation (into an aristocrat dominated by bourgeois standards) is to be signaled by his return to the country. Corrupt Lady Willit, on the other hand, urged on by her fine friends, is totally unwilling to return to a rural existence. "Sure, child," Lady Frankair urges her, "you can never be so tame a domestic animal as to submit to dwell with birds and beasts! The town was built for rational creatures" (II, 229). True enough—but consider Sprightly's observation to Lord Courtlove: "An owl! an ass!—Sure all grave animals are ridiculous—but man. Really, my lord, whenever I see you in this solemn wise way, I shall think of a grave animal; and I must laugh, whatever be the consequences" (II, 239). The country may be the resort of domestic animals—but the "rational creatures" for whom man built the town have degraded themselves to worse than domestic animals, just as the aristocrats have degraded the solid mercantile values. The commerce of Barter and his like is far removed from "the great commerce of the world"—*i.e.*, of the aristocracy—which is bribery. " 'Tis the great commerce of the world: for a man of rank or figure is above selling any thing—but his friend,—or himself" (II, 254). The country may be paradise or hell, depending upon the person who inhabits it—and to the corrupt mind there is little to choose between the two. "I had rather really *die* in town than *live* in the country," remarks Lady Willit; "though I hate paradise, 'tis painted so monstrously like it" (II, 230). Later when she is actually about to leave, Mrs. Buxom observes to her of the country, " 'Tis like hell; 'tis easy to get thither.—But to return,—there's the point" (II, 272).

These excerpts make the play sound more witty and more tightly unified in imagery and theme than it actually is. Although the city-country, aristocrat-bourgeois conflicts indeed dominate the action, the playwright also allows himself frequent excursions into genre representation, like that of the town eclogues; and in such moments his broad purpose seems to disappear. But that purpose itself seems inadequate. The simplicity of the conflict, the purity of the "bad guys" and the "good guys," makes the comedy seem false and weakens any conceivable moral effect. Although the characters and the action of *The Distress'd Wife* partake of the stylization of Restoration comedy, we feel sometimes (as with the character of Barter) that Gay thinks he is depicting real people. As real people these characters are highly unsatisfactory; so is the view of the world that they promulgate, a vision of reality at the opposite pole from that of, say, *The Way of the World.*

The Rehearsal at Goatham, the last and slightest of the posthumous plays, was never acted, nor does this fact represent any loss to the stage. Irving speculates that "Gay wrote it when he was smarting under Walpole's displeasure and angry over the prohibition of *Polly* in 1729,"[34] for it deals with the censorship of a puppet show by the corrupt aldermen of a village. The action is farcical; its only purpose seems to be to express Gay's intense conviction that officialdom is corrupt. For reasons of self-interest, someone decides to block the performance of a puppet show; as a result, when the entrepreneur actually attempts to offer the show, all the local aristocracy see personal reference everywhere; and, although the puppeteer exposes no one, everyone exposes himself before the play is played. The tone is uncharitable and rarely humorous; Gay's bitterness is both unconvincing and unpleasant.

To say that Gay's career as dramatist was much like his career as poet, then, is to refer to his persistent experimentation with form in the effort to find the genre which would make true communication possible, and his recurrent use of certain pet themes and techniques. His plays even more than his poems, however, achieve only qualified success, and the weaker among them are far less interesting than his worst poems. On the other hand, his great triumph was a dramatic one. And it is only in the light of the extraordinary achievement of *The Beggar's Opera* that Gay's literary accomplishment can finally be assessed.

CHAPTER 6

The Beggar's Triumph

IT is, of course, for *The Beggar's Opera* that Gay is remembered in the twentieth century, even among people with no particular interest in eighteenth-century poetry or drama. The play was revived in a rather romanticized London production with great success in 1926; its music was later adapted and presented by Benjamin Britten; in 1963 the Royal Shakespeare Company produced it once more, with great attention to realistic detail, and with a vivid sense of the play's topicality in modern England, once more riddled with scandal in high places. Made into a movie starring Laurence Olivier, *The Beggar's Opera* still returns to art theaters; it has been reissued in formats ranging from an inexpensive student paperback to a splendid reproduction of the 1729 edition; a new recording recently presented all its music and much of its speech.

Probably nothing, however, has brought Gay's work so much to popular attention as the fact that *The Beggar's Opera* was the basis for Bertolt Brecht's *Threepenny Opera,* which relied on it for broad plot structure, for many of its characters, and even for some of its music. The Brecht play, which had a record-breaking run off-Broadway, seems lively and singularly relevant; it has led some readers to new awareness of comparable qualities in Gay's opera, which conveys so highly sophisticated a structure of qualifications that its subject almost seems to be the nature and necessity of qualification in life. In its awareness of the immense difficulty of civilized existence, it speaks directly to our own time.

The relevance of *The Beggar's Opera* to the twentieth century was underlined by its most recent London production, a Brechtian version in which slight textual alterations stressed the applicability of Gay's satire to such modern phenomena as the Profumo affair (*e.g.*, "I, Madam, was once kept by a Tory."). In a "preview" published in the *Manchester Guardian* the day before the play's London opening, Philip Hope-Wallace speculated about the modern effect of the comedy. "Will anyone be shocked now?" he asks, and concludes that it is "a question of age perhaps." "I should think," adds Hope-Wallace, "this indestructible old bag of other men's tunes and its comedy within a comedy would be exactly to modern taste and once again become the talk of the town." [1]

He was, however, rather too optimistic. Although the play's audiences were clearly amused and refreshed by the satiric energy of the "opera" in Peter Wood's production, which employed an elaborate and ingenious set, stylized action, broad parody, and deliberate techniques of "alienation," the newspaper critics were less enthusiastic. They revived the issues of the eighteenth century: the *Sunday Times* commentator, alone in liking the play, praised Polly, like his predecessors two hundred years before, as "an unquenchable sunbeam in a world of tumultuous shadows." [2] Other critics returned to the question of morality. "Morality does not suit an eighteenth-century comedy," wrote David Pryce-Jones, "particularly one so sensitive as *The Beggar's Opera,* where all the lessons to be learnt are implied and all the criticism is self-contained." [3] Kenneth Tynan had similar objections: "What should be implied is shrieked aloud." [4] The problem remains: how can moral satire be made clear and convincing without becoming too blatant? Gay solved that problem largely through his conception of the play; the modern producer, by trying to stress through setting (the play takes place on a prison ship), realistic costume, and stylized action the indictment of social conditions implicit in *The Beggar's Opera,* apparently made that indictment less palatable.

In considering the *Fables* we discovered that the nature of their form helped Gay to achieve success. The same is true of *The Beggar's Opera:* the special variety of dramatic form that Gay here chose was maximally useful in solving the problems that plagued him. He had long experimented with various uses of disguise in drama; now he developed a form almost completely dependent on disguise. He could actually introduce himself directly into his play, given the disguise (and a very significant one it is, considering his preoccupation with money) of beggar.

The importance of this mask as a distancing device becomes apparent when we compare the Introduction of *The Beggar's Opera* with that of its sequel, *Polly*. The first words of the Beggar in the earlier play are these: "If Poverty be a Title to Poetry, I am sure Nobody can dispute mine. I own my self of the Company of Beggars; and I make one at their Weekly Festivals at St. *Gile's*. I have a small Yearly Salary for my Catches, and am welcome to a Dinner there whenever I please, which is more than most Poets can say" (I, 135). The charm of this speech comes chiefly from the fact that the poet thinks of himself *mainly* as beggar, only secondarily as poet; from this perspective he can treat the financial need characteristic of poets with saving irony. He does not appear to take himself or his poetry very seriously; extolling the pleasures of beggarhood, he thus makes a telling comment on the difficulties of being a poet (his point, of course, is that the beggar is *more* independent than the typical poet). But he manages to avoid pathos and distasteful self-concern: his self-esteem is, for a change, appealing rather than unattractive.

His counterpart in *Polly,* on the other hand, is called not *beggar* but *poet*. The disguise is much thinner, and the language of the character reflects his greater closeness to the actual nature of the author: "A Sequel to a play is like more last words. It is a kind of absurdity; and really, sir, you have prevailed upon me to pursue this subject against my judgment. . . . I know, I must have been looked upon as whimsical, and particular, if I had scrupled to have risqued my reputation for my profit; for why should I be more squeamish than my betters? and so, sir, contrary to my opinion, I bring *Polly* once again upon the stage" (II, 3). This is Gay speaking virtually in his own voice. After the wit of the first sentence, the speech degenerates into a sort of apology which upon analysis becomes increasingly distasteful. The point seems to be that the author *is,* in fact, offering this play for the sake of personal profit, but that his mode of admitting this is intended to remove all onus from him. He retains the rather unpleasant tone of moral superiority with no evidence of any real claim to such elevation. One important effect of the series of disguises in *The Beggar's*

Opera is to make all pretensions to superiority into jokes; nothing in *Polly* reveals the Poet's claim as ludicrous. But the joke is necessary; the perspective it provides is a major—perhaps *the* major—source of strength in *The Beggar's Opera.*

Of course the disguise of Beggar for the author is only the first of many masks in *The Beggar's Opera;* all serve similar purposes of implicit commentary. The other disguises in the play are more complicated and less obvious than the introductory one, and they are difficult to define. Is one to say, for example, that Macheath is essentially an aristocrat in the disguise of a highwayman? Or is it more accurate to say that the highwayman in the play disguise themselves to themselves as aristocrats? Here is a sample of dialogue among Macheath's gang:

Ned: Who is there here that would not dye for his Friend?
Harry: Who is there here that would betray him for his Interest?
Matt: Show me a Gang of Courtiers that can say as much.
Ben: We are for a just Partition of the World, for every Man hath a Right to enjoy Life.
Matt: We retrench the Superfluities of Mankind. The World is avaritious, and I hate Avarice. A covetous fellow, like a Jack-daw, steals what he was never made to enjoy, for the sake of hiding it. These are the Robbers of Mankind, for Money was made for the Free-hearted and Generous, and where is the Injury of taking from another, what he hath not the Heart to make use of?

(I, 163-64)

These are aristocrats indeed: honorable, loyal, governed by principle; and if the principles seem to partake largely of rationalization, surely this fact makes the gang seem no less *aristocratic.* We get a different, but equally convincing, view of the highwayman as aristocrat from the Peachums, who, as William Empson has demonstrated, represent the bourgeois perspective in the play.

Mrs. Peachum: I knew she was always a proud Slut; and now the wench hath play'd the Fool and married, because forsooth she would do like the Gentry. Can you support the Expense of a Husband, Hussy, in gaming, drinking and whoring? . . . If you must be married, could you introduce no-body into our Family but a Highwayman? Why, thou foolish Jade, thou wilt be as ill-us'd, and as much neglected, as if thou hadst married a Lord!

Peachum: Let not your Anger, my Dear, break through the Rules of Decency, for the Captain looks upon himself in the Military Capacity, as a Gentleman by his Profession.

(I, 149)

Earlier, before the marriage is revealed, the Peachums discuss Macheath's wealth and prospects. They agree that he keeps good company and associates with the gentry, but this tendency is a weakness: he cannot expect to win at the gaming tables without the education of a fine gentleman. "What business hath he to keep Company with Lords and Gentlemen?" Mrs. Peachum concludes: "he should leave them to prey upon one another" (I, 142). To be aristocrats means, then, in this world, *not* to be men of honor and principle, but to be men who prey on one another.

William Hazlitt, assuming the identity between aristocrat and gentleman, finds Macheath heroic indeed:

> Macheath should be a fine man and a gentleman, but he should be one of God Almighty's gentlemen, not a gentleman of the black rod. His gallantry and good-breeding should arise from impulse, not from rule; not from the trammels of education, but from a soul generous, courageous, good-natured, aspiring, amorous. The class of the character is very difficult to hit. It is something between gusto and slang, like port-wine and brandy mixed. It is not the mere gentleman that should be represented, but the blackguard sublimated into the gentleman. This character is qualified in a highwayman, as it is qualified in a prince. We hope this is not a libel.[5]

This image of Macheath as nature's nobleman is appealing, but the play will not allow us to rest content with it. Just at the point where we may be tempted to say that the highwaymen are true aristocrats, the nobility false ones, we discover that Macheath, for example, despite his prating of honor, is as capable of treachery, as proud of his seductions and their ultimate effect in populating Drury Lane (the resort of prostitutes) as his "betters" could conceivably be.

Similarly, our vision of Polly is made to fluctuate wildly. Eighteenth-century audiences wept and applauded at Polly's song, "Oh ponder well! be not severe," responding to its pathos and to her as a pathetic heroine. She has, to be sure, all the postures of the traditional romantic lead: her frequent evocations of the idea of love, her parroting of the notions of playbooks (although, to be sure, her admission of their source rather tempers the potency of such notions), her quite unjustified faith in Macheath's loyalty and her unwillingness to betray him—all these characteristics are conventionally admirable. But the first words of this Polly, who insists on her sentimentality and her virtue, spoken to her father, are, "I know as well as any of the fine Ladies how to make the most of my self and my Man too. A Woman knows how to be mercenary, though she hath never been in a Court or at an Assembly. We have it in our Natures, Papa" (I, 147).

This is not, to be sure, a direct statement of Polly's own feelings: she wishes at the moment to obscure her actual marriage to Macheath by pretending to conform precisely to her father's standards. But she has the lesson a bit too pat for comfort: it is easy to suspect that she really partakes of these values. After all, the truth is that she *does,* as she claims, have such visible marks of the captain's favor as a watch. The song she sings immediately after this speech ("Virgins are like the fair Flower in its Lustre") emphasizes the commodity view of virginity; when, later in the play, Polly comes into contact with Lucy, who has loved not wisely but too well, her sense of superiority rests on the fact that she has been smart enough to make a better bargain than Lucy: marriage for virginity. William Empson documents her feverish interest in hanging, the extent to which she seems almost to desire what she most fears, Macheath's death by hanging, the only form which death takes in this play.

All this is not to say that Polly lacks charm; she is, of course, the play's most appealing character. But it is the nature of this play that its most charming personages are frequently undercut, while its least attractive figures have moments of such moral clarity that we can hardly reject them. Thus the senior Peachums, underhanded, self-seeking, treacherous as they are, can convince us momentarily that the evils they abundantly demonstrate are merely natural concomitants of good business practice: they have the airs, the language, the self-esteem of successful businessmen; and our moral detestation of them cannot be quite secure—particularly if we perceive their resemblance to modern representatives of the business world. All the characters of *The Beggar's Opera* could be transferred to a new plot about the participants in a television quiz-show scandal with little change in their natures or their comments. The play leaves us with no secure stance; in place of one perspective from which to view the characters, it offers many. These characters do not come on stage in the casing of a mummy or a crocodile. They are disguised even *from themselves;* they do not know what they really are. As a consequence it becomes difficult for us to know what they are. This is a far more subtle use of the disguise motif than Gay ever made before or later; it dramatizes the almost metaphysical implications of the device.

II

If the shifting self-disguises (Polly as her father's daughter, as sentimental heroine, as wronged wife; Macheath as honorable gentleman, as dishonorable seducer; the Peachums as practical business people, as despicable profiteers in vice) afford one mode of constant qualification in the play, another is provided by the patterns of imagery which run through songs and prose alike. William Empson has discussed brilliantly and in some detail the imagery of hanging and its ramifications. Two other themes of the imagery are almost equally obvious: money and animals. And the three patterns in conjunction provide interesting commentary on one another.

The image of human beings as animals, a favorite of Gay's, becomes in *The Beggar's Opera* a subtle and complicated device. Lockit's direct summary of the motif is well-known: "Lions, Wolves, and Vulturs don't live together in Herds, Droves or Flocks.—Of all Animals of Prey, Man is the only sociable one. Every one of us preys upon his Neighbour, and yet we herd together.—*Peachum* is my Companion, my Friend—According to the Custom of the World, indeed, he may quote thousands of Precedents for cheating me—And shall I not make use of the Privilege of Friendship to make him a Return?" (I, 196). In tone and emphasis this speech is wonderfully characteristic of the play. It parodies the note of self-satisfaction we hear so often in these characters: Lockit is smug over the "superiority" of man, demonstrated by his sociability, to other vicious animals with an immediate exposition of precisely what this sociability means in practice. But the play provides many more specific statements of the similarity between men and animals.

It seems—although there are many exceptions—that the women in the play are somewhat more likely to think of love in animal terms, while the men connect love directly with money. Mrs. Peachum sees the "simple Maid" as a moth, constantly playing about the flame until, if she is not made a wife, her honor's singed. ("If Love the Virgin's Heart invade" [I, 143]). Polly describes the virgin as a flower, with her lovers as bees and butterflies ("Virgins are like the fair Flower in its Lustre" [I, 147]). Later, in a sentimental song, she likens herself to a turtledove ("The Turtle thus with plaintive crying" [I, 156]). Again, immediately after Macheath, masculine and money-oriented, has compared his love for her to that of a miser for his shilling, she compares hers for him to that of a boy for his sparrow ("The Miser thus a Shilling sees" [I, 162]). Jenny Diver, one of the trulls, sees Macheath as a cock attended by hens ("Before the Barn-door crowing" [I, 171]).

All these images, with the possible exception of Polly's boy-sparrow one, are comparatively innocent, although in the total context of the play they seem less so than we might expect. Gradually, though, the connections between human love and the animal world become increasingly sinister. Macheath, betrayed by women, shifts the bird imagery to a new realm: "Women are Decoy Ducks; who can trust them! Beasts, Jades, Jilts, Harpies, Furies, Whores!" (I, 173). When Lucy confronts her betrayer, Macheath, in prison, she sings a song which makes him the trapped rat and her the good housewife who throws it to the dog or cat ("Thus when a good Huswife sees a Rat," [I, 177]). Polly, still dwelling on bird imagery, compares herself to a female, Macheath to a male swallow, in a song whose point, Empson suggests, is that she is eagerly awaiting Macheath's death ("Thus when the Swallow, seeking Prey" [I, 186]).[6] Then Lucy sees herself as a fox, Macheath as another ("I like the Fox shall grieve" [I, 193]). The final two songs in this sequence of animal lyrics are worth quoting in full. The first is sung by Lockit to Peachum, as he suggests that Macheath can be trapped by keeping an eye on Polly:

What Gudgeons are we Men!
Ev'ry Woman's easy Prey.
Though we have felt the Hook, agen
We bite and they betray.
The Bird that hath been trapt,
When he hears his calling Mate,
To her he flies, again he's clapt
Within the wiry Grate.
(I, 201-02)

The second is sung alternately by Polly and Lucy:

Polly: A Curse attends that Woman's Love.
Who always would be pleasing.
Lucy: The Pertness of the billing Dove,
Like tickling, is but teazing.
Polly: What then in Love can Woman do?
Lucy: If we grow fond they shun us.
Polly: And when we fly them, they pursue:
Lucy: But leave us when they've won us.
(I, 209)

The songs comment tellingly on the sentimentality of some of the previous uses of bird imagery. Lockit's lyrics are particularly explicit, juxtaposing the image of men as "poor fish" to be hooked by women with an even more sinister picture of female birds as decoys to trap the males. All attempts to glamorize the notion of human beings as animals or birds must ultimately fail; this is degrading imagery, and Lockit, for the moment at least, sees it quite explicitly as such. (It is also Lockit, incidentally, who provides the most menacing animal image of the play: "Like Pikes, lank with Hunger, who miss of their Ends,/ They bite their Companions, and prey on their Friends" [I, 197].) Polly and Lucy, from the opposite, feminine, point of view, perceive the same truth: they may try to romanticize their roles, but the actuality is hard and inescapable.

The pattern of animal imagery, in other words, provides its own commentary. Moving in general from benign to vicious images, it also moves from the unself-conscious, romantic, and conventional to a more cynical and analytical use of the same sort of material. And the later usages reflect back on the earlier ones, causing us to feel that innocence in this world (whatever innocence Polly truly had at first) can be equated only with ignorance, that romanticism is a resource only for those who know nothing of reality.

The notion of human beings as animals is further illuminated by frequent metaphorical and literal remarks about money. Love and money are, of course, closely related: Filch's first song establishes the nature of the relationship:

> 'Tis Woman that seduces all Mankind,
> By her we first were taught the wheedling Arts:
> Her very eyes can cheat; when most she's kind,
> She tricks us of our Money with our Hearts.
> For her, like Wolves by night we roam for Prey,
> And practise ev'ry Fraud to bribe her Charms;
> For Suits of Love, like Law, are won by Pay,
> And Beauty must be fee'd into our Arms.
> (I, 139)

This song not only summarizes the masculine point of view toward "love," as it exists in the world of the play; it also suggests the relation between human emphasis on money and the notion of human beings as animals. Men become wolves, Filch says quite explicitly, because of the feminine demand for money. And since, as other songs and comments in the play make abundantly clear, virtually *every* human enterprise depends upon money, it is quite apparent that man can hardly escape reduction to animality.

Mrs. Peachum is the only woman in the play who states explicitly that women themselves are commodities of equivalent value to money. She sees the maid as "like the golden Oar,/ Which hath Guineas intrinsical in't"; the precise value of the ore is unknown until it is minted. The wife, on the other hand, is "like a Guinea in Gold,/Stampt with the Name of her Spouse"; although she no longer has the advantage of being of incalculable value, she acquires a new benefit: that of being an accepted medium of exchange, "current in every House" (I, 145). "The first time a Woman is frail, she should be somewhat nice methinks, for then or never is the time to make her fortune" (I, 151). This is Mrs. Peachum's morality, and, if no other woman quite states it, there is little evidence that anyone has an essentially different standard. Polly sees Macheath as her "treasure"; she also seems to have had a good sense of the value of her virginity, though she would not use such crass terms as her mother.

"You might sooner tear a Pension out of the Hands of a Courtier, a Fee from a Lawyer, a pretty Woman from a Looking-glass, or any Woman from Quadrille.—But to tear me from thee is impossible!" This is Macheath's idea of a fitting protestation of love to Polly (I, 160), who, in the play's comedy, accepts it quite blandly as such. More consistently than anyone else, he connects love with money. His metaphor of Polly as the shilling, himself as the miser, seems surprising: more often he values women in terms of guineas: "A Man who loves Money, might as well be contented with one Guinea, as I with one Woman" (I, 166). And again, "I must have Women. There is nothing unbends the Mind like them. Money is not so strong a Cordial for the Time" (I, 167).

Hazlitt may include Macheath's "amorousness" among his virtues, but this particular aspect of the captain's high regard for women is hardly attractive. The trulls he has sent to Drury Lane share his values: one praises another because, "Though her Fellow be never so agreeable, she can pick his Pocket as cooly, as if Money were her only Pleasure. Now that is a Command of the Passions uncommon in a Woman!" (I, 170). After one of them betrays the captain (for money), they argue over their "accounts": how many hanged men should be laid to the credit of each (I, 174). Macheath himself is greeted in prison by Lucy, whom he has seduced and left pregnant; one of her songs to him ends:

> Whoever steals a Shilling,
> Through Shame the Guilt conceals:
> In Love the perjur'd Villain
> With Boasts the Theft reveals.
> (I, 178)

And there is justice in her complaint. Macheath convinces her that he plans to marry her, but she is unable to soften her father's heart. Macheath suggests that in such a case a bribe is indicated: "Money well tim'd, and properly apply'd, will do any thing" (I, 184). His next song elaborates the point, concluding that the way to win a woman is to offer her money:

"That Reason with all is prevailing" (185). "In the Account of Love you are in my debt," Macheath tells Lucy (192). "Owe thy Life to me," Lucy replies. But as Macheath points out a bit later, "Death is a Debt,/A Debt on demand" (217)— and a gentleman always pays debts of this sort, if not those of love.

Of course these examples in the play do not even begin to exhaust the discussion of money, its function and its effects. But the ways in which money is connected with love—or with what passes for love in the play—are particularly indicative of the total corruption of the world described here. Filch makes a living by "helping the Ladies to a Pregnancy against their being called down to Sentence" (198)—by eighteenth-century law pregnant women could not be hanged. Sven Armens comments accurately on this fact: "Here sexual intercourse, which can be the warm expression of true love, has been most thoroughly debased. Even lust itself has been undermined. Love is moral and practical; lust is immoral and impractical; but begetting illegitimate children in order to cheat justice combines immorality with a sort of practicality. This is sex as simply business for all concerned; a breed farm for criminals represents the complete perversion of the chivalric code of courtly love."[7]

Except for Polly, sex seems to be hardly more than business for anyone in the play; even Lucy, who claims to be desperately in love, is capable of bargaining over her sexual rights. The Peachums consider their daughter a business asset; Polly herself can deal with her virginity as a commodity; Macheath makes little distinction between the pursuits of love and of money; Lockit thinks of love and money as equivalent material for bargaining. The money-love imagery sums up and emphasizes the nature of a society completely dominated by money—for frequent references in the play insist that lawyers, courtiers, doctors—all the world—care only for money; and Lockit and Peachum, those companions in crime, fall out before our eyes over their profits.

"Money well tim'd, and properly apply'd, will do any thing." "Of all Animals of Prey, Man is the only sociable one." Considered in conjunction, these two thematic statements explain and reflect upon one another. The cause of man's preying and of his sociability, as expounded in this play, is money. Or, conversely, the reason that money will do anything is that man is an animal of prey. His prey is only incidentally other human beings, ultimately it is money. Fierce punitive measures dispose of the weak, the poor, the unlucky in such a society: this brings us to the matter of hanging, the source of the third major pattern of imagery. Love, death, and money; human beings reducing themselves to a sub-animal level—it sounds a somber play indeed. And of course it *is* somber—but funny as well; for the involved structure of cross-commentary, keeping the reader constantly a little off-balance, forces him to see the ridiculous as well as the horrible aspects of each situation.

The ending of the play is a perfect instance of the way in which this particular double view (of the world as both horrifying and ridiculous) is maintained. Macheath is about to be hanged when the player of the Introduction protests to the beggar-author that an opera must end happily. The beggar agrees to cry a reprieve for Macheath; the player approves: "All this we must do, to comply with the Taste of the Town" (223). Sven Armens summarizes the implications of this piece of action by observing, "The moral of the play is dismissed as the town in its ethical degradation dismisses morality."[8] True enough—here is the horror: that the "town" which witnesses the play is a society of the same sort as that depicted in the play equally corrupt, equally perverted in values, and that honest drama, which shows "that the lower Sort of People have their Vices in a degree as well as the Rich: and that they are punish'd for them" (224), is consequently impossible. But it is equally true (and of course Sven Armens elsewhere demonstrates his awareness of the play's comic aspects) that the superb inconsequence of the ending accords tonally with the general lightheartedness of the play as a whole, lightheartedness which persists, paradoxically, despite the bitterness, the intense cynicism reiterated by the ending. It is quite proper to laugh at these matters—if one can retain the perspective of an outsider and fail to realize that he also is being condemned. And it is proper also to abhor and denounce the world depicted: the one response is incomplete without the other.

III

An obvious aspect of *The Beggar's Opera* which we will in the main have to ignore is its music. Most operas, even comic operas, hardly exist for the average reader outside their stage productions; their music supplies justification or compensation for the improbabilities of their plots, their eccentricities of language and meter. It is a measure of how remarkable Gay's accomplishment was that his play has such vivid life even on the printed page, its songs self-justified by the charm of their lyrics. But the music of *The Beggar's Opera* adds an extra dimension to the play on stage—and Gay used this resource, too, in his elaborate structure of cross-commentary.

The commentary comes from the relation of Gay's lyrics to the original words attached to the music. Almost all the songs in the play are traditional tunes (hence the name of the genre created by this work: *ballad opera*), and the lyrics originally connected with them would have been familiar to the early audiences. A recent edition of the play has printed texts of the early songs side by side with Gay's versions,[9] and some comparisons are instructive. Many have been pointed out by Professor Bronson in the essay previously cited. In general, they intensify the same implications we have discovered already. When Mrs. Peachum sings of how maids are like gold ore, wives like gold guineas, she sings to a tune which earlier had words insisting that:

> We're just like a Mouse in a Trap,
> Or Vermin caught in a Gin;
> We Sweat and Fret, and try to Escape
> And Curse the sad Hour we came in.

Thus the imagery of money is in effect placed in conjunction with that of animals—the precise metaphor of the mouse in a trap is to be used later by Lucy. The song, " 'Tis Woman that seduces all Mankind" goes with a tune whose words describe a masculine seducer who loves and leaves his victims: if listeners are conscious of the traditional version, they are by this very fact prevented from having a simple view of the situation. Macheath's sentimental song, "Pretty Polly, say," is based on a piece beginning "Pretty Parret say"—and this in itself is adequate comment on the captain's sentimentality. (Indeed, the view of Polly as parrot sheds light on her apparent complexity: her ideas are secondhand, derived from diverse sources; she recites whatever seems appropriate in a specific situation.) The lyric beginning, "No power on earth can e'er divide/The knot that sacred Love hath ty'd" must be considered in conjunction with its predecessor:

> Remember Damon you did tell,
> In Chastity you lov'd me well,
> But now alas I am undone,
> And here am left to make my Moan.

So much for professions of everlasting and sacred love!

These sketchy examples should be enough to emphasize once more the consistency with which Gay insisted upon keeping his readers and audiences simultaneously conscious of different—often radically different—perspectives on the action, the characters, the very language of his play. *The Beggar's Opera* is a work of enormous sophistication, unprecedented in Gay's literary career and never again to be equaled or even approached by him. When he attempted immediately to duplicate his success by reusing the same characters in *Polly*, the result was a literary—although by no means a financial—fiasco. And perhaps the best way to conclude a discussion of *The Beggar's Opera* is by a brief examination of its sequel, which demonstrates by its failure to employ them how valuable the devices of the earlier play are.

IV

The early history of *Polly* is more interesting than the play itself. The comedy was finished late in 1728. Although it was far more innocent politically than *The Beggar's Opera*, in December its performance was prohibited on vague political grounds by the lord chamberlain. (As Gay himself put it, "I am accused, in general terms, of having written many disaffected libels and seditious pamphlets."[10]) W. E. Schultz suggests the probability that the prohibition depended not so much on the content of the play as on the fact "that the report of a new play bearing Gay's name was . . . unfit for the comfort of the Walpole circle."[11] At any rate, the play could be printed if not acted, with the prospect of the added sales that censorship always seems to bring. Within a year 10,500 copies had been sold of two large quarto editions.[12] Estimates of Gay's actual proceeds vary wildly: Schultz believes that the playwright may have made £3,000;[13] James Sutherland suggests £1,000.[14] At any rate, immediate pirated editions reduced his receipts: the first piracies appeared within three or four days after the original publication of *Polly*, early in April, 1729, and by June there were injunctions for piracy against seventeen printers and booksellers.[15] Evidently a good many others felt, with Gay, that a sequel to *The Beggar's Opera* could hardly fail.

But, whatever its receipts, the play remains a failure. *The Beggar's Opera* presents us with a world in which *everyone* is corrupt: we may discern differences of degree, but no real distinctions of kind. Filch, the youth who makes his living by causing pregnancies, has his moments of charm; Polly, that delightful heroine, has hers of unpleasant calculation. In *Polly*, on the other hand, society splits into heroes and villains; there is no doubt at all where one's sympathies are to lie. Polly has become a model of virtue; we are expected to take with entire seriousness her protestations of undying love to Macheath, although at the end of the play, having discovered Macheath's full villainy, she appears ready to marry a noble savage who is also, conveniently, a prince.

Her speech at this juncture is characteristic of her language throughout: "I am charm'd, prince, with your generosity and virtue. 'Tis only by the pursuit of those we secure real happiness. Those that know and feel virtue in themselves, must love it in others. Allow me to give a decent time to my sorrows. But my misfortunes at present interrupt the joys of victory" (II, 78). It is almost inconceivable that Gay could offer us such speech with no ironic perspective, but here and throughout the play he does exactly that. The Indians are without exception noble, so their language must be noble, too; the pirates, invariably villainous, talk always like villains.

Macheath has now painted himself black (a convenient symbol), named himself *Morano*, and taken up with Jenny Diver, who managed to be transported with him. He is no longer the model of the highwayman-gentleman, having been morally destroyed by his unworthy love. When at the end he is finally hanged, we could hardly wish for a reprieve (indeed, one is actually granted, but too late): he has become so conventionally detestable that we find him both boring and distasteful and feel well rid of him. ("If justice hath overtaken him," says the Indian prince to Polly, with superb lack of logic, "he was unworthy of you" [II, 76].) The only interesting villain in the play is a minor one, Ducat, the plantation owner who originally buys Polly to be his concubine and who at the very last hopes still to make a profit from her. In Gay's depiction of him alone (and occasionally of Mrs. Trapes, a transplant from *The Beggar's Opera*), we find touches of the poet's old satiric insight.

It is significant that these minor figures should be the most successful characters in the play, for they are also the two who have the closest relation to eighteenth-century actuality. Ducat is struggling to follow the model of the English gentleman; Mrs. Trapes, his tutor, guides him in his progress in vice. Given this much relation to real society, these characters seem more meaningful than their companions; the Indians, the pirates, Macheath himself, certainly Polly, do not have much to do with reality, although the playwright frequently insists that Macheath and his band are allegorical representatives of the viciousness inherent in English society. In *The Beggar's Opera,* on the other hand, although the atmosphere is permeated with a delicious sense of unreality (we don't believe for a moment that highwaymen or "fences" ever talked like that; we don't believe in the action; the sudden shift at the ending is a surprise but not a shock, considering that none of the action has caused the suspension of disbelief), the total effect depends fundamentally on our constant, steady conviction that everything that happens on stage has its direct analogue on higher levels of society. Lacking the power to convey this conviction, *Polly* can only seem an essentially frivolous and meaningless exercise.

There's no use flogging a dead horse, and *Polly* is a very dead one indeed. Yet it provides a dramatic illustration of how precarious was the balance Gay established in *The Beggar's Opera.* Lacking that balance all other devices must fail. The imagery in *Polly* comes from the same realms as that of its predecessor; the songs are based on similar originals. But nothing works in *Polly,* and certainly no two devices work together. The difference between hackwork and comic drama informed by a vision can seldom have been so clearly demonstrated as in the relation between *The Beggar's Opera* and its sequel.

CHAPTER 7

Fitting the Mask

IN thinking of the work of John Gay as a whole, we are forced to the conclusion already implicit in our treatment of the individual poems and plays: that we are faced with a particularly complex case of an artistic talent not entirely in tune with its public expression. If the conventions of his time directed Gay toward a valuable increase of complexity, they may also have forced him into modes of poetic expression not fully representative of his talent. "Only after death, only in solitude, does a man's true nature emerge," wrote Franz Kafka. ". . . Then it can be seen who did the more harm, his contemporaries to him, or he to his contemporaries. If the latter, he was a great man." Gay was not, in this sense, a great man. His sense of fresh literary possibilities exerted no apparent influence on his contemporaries. The charm, grace and delicacy of *Dione*, expressed only in isolated passages, never fully realized, suggest possible new directions for poetry. But Gay appears never even to have completely recognized his own special gifts; certainly he never made them impressive to the critics of his time. Instead, he allowed his contemporaries to dictate the forms he would use—directly (almost all his literary enterprises were suggested by someone else) and indirectly, through unarticulated pressures. Satire was certainly not his natural vein, yet at it he doggedly labored. His greatest success, *The Beggar's Opera*, was triumphant in precisely the mode most admired by Pope and Swift; but it involved the rejection of Gay's gentler talents.

The process of acquiring sophistication, in more than twenty years of poetic development, was clearly for Gay an arduous one, and he only sporadically achieved the goal of authority combined with deftness. His failures as well as his successes, however, illuminate for us the nature of certain vital poetic problems in the eighteenth century. A towering poet like Pope solves such problems so expertly that we may be hardly aware of their existence; Gay, by his struggles, makes us acutely conscious of the special demands which an age of firm standards might make of its poets.

It was assumed in the early eighteenth century that poets were truth-sayers. The function of poetry was not simply to entertain or to create beauty or wit; it was (and this idea, of course, rests on a long and distinguished tradition) to delight *and* to instruct. Instruction was rather more important than delight—a fact which we may forget in our own delight with the wit and verve of eighteenth-century poetry at its best. "Poetry . . . is an Art, by which a Poet excites Passion (and for that very cause entertains Sense) in order to satisfie and improve, to delight and reform the Mind, and so to make Mankind happier and better," wrote John Dennis,[1] whose sense of the high seriousness of the poet's responsibility is repeatedly echoed.

In the context of such an exalted view of the poet's responsibility, the man who would make poetry a profession must have more resources than verbal dexterity and a sound education. It is not surprising that eighteenth-century poetry is so conspicuously dominated by *personae.* Not only for the satirist was the pose of authority necessary: the poetry of direct moral statement, even the poetry of feeling, needed the dignity of the seer's voice to justify it. For the poet was not simply, as Wordsworth would have him be, a man speaking to men; he was far more significantly a teacher, sometimes almost a prophet, a man meaningfully *removed* from other men. Such, at any rate, he must for purposes of his poetry pretend to be.

In *Wine, The Fan, Rural Sports,* even *The Shepherd's Week,* it does not seem fanciful to discern the voice of a poet trying to *dodge* responsibility for what he had to say, attempting to disappear behind various conventional disguises. There is nothing unusual in the fact that Gay began his poetic career relying heavily on classical models. Pope's first published poems (written, of course, when he was a great deal younger than the Gay of *Rural Sports* or *The Shepherd's Week*) were Virgilian pastorals; it is difficult to distinguish in them any individual Popean note. Yet the problem of evaluting Pope's pastorals is entirely different from that of evaluating Gay's. In Pope's pieces we discern absolute clarity of intention: the pastorals are pure, entirely themselves, clearly implying definite poetic values and standards. Gay's may seem "fresher," less completely imitative, but they possess no equivalent clarity. In them Virgilian imitation constantly slips into Virgilian parody.

The standards implied by parody (realism, for example: parody of Virgil's pastorals is for Gay partly a way of criticizing the Latin poet's evocation of a country life that never existed) are contradicted by those implicit in imitation (where, for example, aesthetic beauty becomes a poetic criterion). Gay's knowledge of country life wars with his suspicion that such matters are hardly worth knowing about; his sense of rural charm conflicts with his awareness of rural crudity. His choice of pseudo-Miltonic or pseudo-georgic or pseudo-pastoral as a technique for conveying his ideas amounts to an avoidance of those ideas: the voice of Milton (or the parody voice of anti-Milton) implies an established set of attitudes within a rather limited range, and no such "set" really coincided with Gay's own feelings. He used, then, a pose of literary sophistication to escape the necessity of conveying and resolving the actual complexity of his feelings; he presented, in effect, a mask itself, instead of a man looming behind one.

In *Trivia* and the verse epistles the relation between poet and *persona* is less strained, but we sense increasingly Gay's discomfort at wearing a mask at all. The echoes of Virgil in *Trivia* are valuable; when georgic parody is applied to the affairs of city rather than of country, implications of complexity are in effect "built in" to the device. The values of the country are thus automatically placed in juxtaposition with those of the city; constant comment and cross-evaluation are implied. In the epistles, on the other hand, Gay largely (although not entirely) discarded the technique of direct imitation or parody of classical models; he attempted to adopt the less specific voice of poet as critic and commentator.

But we discovered in both instances the extent to which the poet repeatedly found himself trapped by his own direct involvement with his material. James Sutherland describes as one of Gay's poetic merits his ability to turn a real scene into a delicately artificial construct.[2] This is certainly one of Gay's important skills—but its corollary is that the artificial for him constantly wavers toward the real: he evokes the potential delicacy and charm of a London scene, then believes in and loves his own creation. Of course one does not demand of a poet a simple point of view—quite the contrary. There is no reason to object to the fact that Gay, in *Trivia,* also constantly *criticizes* the modern city by contrasting it implicitly with the virtuous country and the more virtuous past. The objection must be, rather, that his poetic resources still do not seem adequate to the multiplicity of his values. When he tries to summon the authority of the poet as critic of civilization, his voice falters; the critic disappears in the lover of civilization, or blusters unconvincingly in an effort to assert values not fully or deeply felt. Similarly in the epistles: Gay as critic disintegrates into Gay as participant-observer, too much involved in his own follies to find folly morally detestable, although perfectly capable of chuckling at himself and at the rest of the world.

Such criticism of Gay's poetry should not be allowed to obscure the fact that even his earliest pieces seem largely self-justifying by their charm alone. Indeed we can hardly wish for *Trivia,* say, to have more moral weight: its delicacy, precision, humor might easily disappear if the critic's fervor were more intense. We may have similar feelings about the early plays: they please by their quality of *jeu d'esprit.* Aware of their inadequacies, their weaknesses of structure, their various failures of moral clarity, we must suspect that such weaknesses could not be eliminated without corresponding loss of charm.

Gay's most successful works, *The Beggar's Opera* and the first series of *Fables,* seem the more interesting in the light of his many qualified successes. In them, of course, charm coexists with moral intensity, but that intensity may be of a highly complicated variety. In them Gay has mastered the use of a *persona.* In his earliest works, the *personae* he relied on most were extremely sophisticated: he would be the highly literate imitator-parodist of the rural bard and simultaneously of Virgil, or the citizen of the world commenting on Paris in implicit or explicit juxtaposition with London. In the later, better works, on the other hand, Gay employed the *persona* of simple man. There is a vast difference between the genre of fable and that of Virgilian parody, just as between the disguise of world citizen and that of beggar. Pretending to be simpler than he really was (merely to tell a little moral tale, or merely to comply with the taste of an audience) Gay found it possible to reveal and to order his own complexity; pretending to be sophisticated, he might come perilously close to chaos of values. He finally learned to manipulate his mask rather than hide behind it.

His great successes were satiric, yet we must continue to say that satire was not his bent. There is too much evidence that his special talents lay elsewhere. If we cannot wish for the fervor of the committed critic to obscure the delicate observations of the man of warm feeling, it is because, in the last analysis, Gay achieves his particularity not, like Pope, from uncompromising intelligence, but rather from his fundamental cleverness and his emotional integrity—the instincts of the entertainer and of the lyric singer—made gradually to subordinate themselves and to become instruments of moral perception. In *Dione,* for example, one glimpses the pure lyric appreciation of the beauties of the countryside which persists in Gay's work throughout his pilgrimage toward satiric respectability. In *Trivia,* on the other hand, there is an almost equivalently fundamental and intense response to the beauty of high civilization, a response obscured again and again by the obligation the poet feels to treat the town in a critical vein. In *The Beggar's Opera,* in the *Fables,* our reaction is technically a reaction to satire, but the satire is animated less by moral fervor than by a bittersweet perception of the persistent follies of the race. An age of wit must insist on the promulgation and defense of intellectual standards of excellence. John Gay rarely managed to meet completely the standards of his time, but he suggests—and this is his greatest interest for the critic of eighteenth-century literature—a variety of ways in which a highly individual sensibility might operate even within so established a context.

Notes and References

Chapter One

1. Samuel Johnson, "J. Philips," *Lives of the English Poets,* ed. George B. Hill, 3 vols. (Oxford, 1905), II, 284-85.
2. John M. Aden, "The 1720 Version of *Rural Sports* and the Georgic Tradition," *Modern Language Quarterly,* XX (1959,) 228-32.
3. Pope to Gay, Aug. 23, 1713, *The Correspondence of Alexander Pope,* ed. George Sherburn, 5 vols. (Oxford, 1956), I, 188.
4. Oct. 28, 1710; Pope, *Correspondence,* I, 101.
5. The essays were in Numbers 22, 23, 28, 30, and 32 of the *Guardian.*
6. Pope, *Correspondence,* I, 229.
7. Hoyt Trowbridge, "Pope, Gay, and *The Shepherd's Week,*" *Modern Language Quarterly,* V (1944), 79-88.
8. *Ibid.*, pp. 84-86.
9. John Robert Moore, "Gay's Burlesque of Sir Richard Blackmore's Poetry," *Journal of English and Germanic Philology,* L (1951), 83-89.
10. William D. Ellis, Jr., "Thomas D'Urfey, the Pope-Philips Quarrel, and *The Shepherd's Week,*" *Publications of the Modern Language Association,* LXXIV (1959), 203-12.
11. J. E. Congleton, *Theories of Pastoral Poetry in England, 1684-1798* (Gainesville, Fla., 1952), p. 93.
12. Samuel Johnson, "Gay," *Lives of the English Poets,* II, 61.
13. Bonamy Dobree, *English Literature in the Early Eighteenth Century* (Oxford, 1959), p. 141.
14. William Henry Irving, *John Gay, Favorite of the Wits* (Durham, N.C., 1940), p. 83.
15. *The Poetical Works of John Gay,* ed. G. C. Faber (London, 1926), p. 29. The whole poem is highly illuminating and well worth reading.
16. Sven M. Armens, *John Gay, Social Critic* (New York, 1954), p. 167.
17. Hoyt Trowbridge, *op. cit.,* p. 84.

Chapter Two

1. William Henry Irving, *op. cit.,* p. 127.
2. Sven M. Armens, *op. cit.,* 87.

3. March 13, 1731/2; Pope, *Correspondence,* III, 277.

4. The word *trivia* derives from the Latin *trivialis,* "of the cross-roads," hence, "commonplace," which in turn comes from *trivium,* "place where three roads meet" (*tri,* "three," plus *via,* "road").

5. It would be misleading to imply that the *Georgics* provided Gay's *only* model for *Trivia.* For subject matter the poem is also indebted to Juvenal, Persius, and Horace. But Gay's transformation of Juvenal, for example, into a modern guise is perfectly conventional, the same sort of exercise practiced by many of his contemporaries. His treatment of Virgil is much more original, and significant in its originality: Gay's choice of a country poem as model for one on the city helped most importantly to make possible the expression of his own sense of ambiguity.

6. For a full discussion of the tradition, see Dwight Durling, *Georgic Tradition in English Poetry* (New York, 1935). P. M. Spacks, *The Varied God: A Critical Study of Thomson's "The Seasons"* (Berkeley, Calif., 1959) provides a detailed analysis of the confused values expressed through one of the eighteenth century's most extensive georgic imitations.

7. James Sutherland, "John Gay," *Eighteenth Century English Literature: Modern Essays in Criticsm* (New York, 1959), p. 138.

8. Virgil, *Georgics* (Dryden's translation), II, 720-25, 728-31.

9. Sutherland, *op. cit.,* p. 138.

Chapter Three

Portions of this and the succeeding Chapter appeared, in different form, in my article entitled "John Gay: A Satirist's Progress," *Essays in Criticism,* XIV (1964), 156-70.

1. William Henry Irving, *op. cit.,* p. 181.

2. Poems eliminated included *Wine,* some translations of Ovid, and a group of translations from Ariosto written that year and not printed elsewhere. See *ibid.,* p. 178.

3. Maynard Mack, "The Muse of Satire," *Studies in the Literature of the Augustan Age,* ed. Richard C. Boys (Ann Arbor, Michigan, 1952), p. 224.

4. *Ibid.,* pp. 227-28.

5. Sven M. Armens, *op. cit.,* p. 119.

6. *Ibid.,* pp. 116-17, 118.

7. See Basil Williams, *The Whig Supremacy, 1714-1760* (Oxford, 1952), pp. 169-70.

8. See Irving, *op. cit.,* pp. 110-11.

9. Armens, *op. cit.,* pp. 110-11.

10. *Ibid.,* p. 169.

11. Faber, *op. cit.*, p. 131.
12. James Sutherland, *op. cit.*, p. 139.

Chapter Four

1. William Henry Irving, *op. cit.*, p. 222.
2. James Sutherland, *op. cit.*, p. 138.
3. Irving, *op. cit.*, p. 221.
4. Henry W. Wells, "The Seven Against London," *Sewanee Review*, XLVII (1939), 518.
5. Duncan C. Tovey, "John Gay," *Reviews and Essays in English Literature* (London, 1897), p. 133.
6. Quoted by Irving, *op. cit.*, p. 220.
7. Joseph Warton, *An Essay on the Genius and Writings of Pope*, Vol. II (London, 1782), 314-15.
8. *European Magazine*, LXIX (January, 1816), pp. 29-30.
9. *Ibid.*, LXIX (May, 1816), p. 416.
10. *Ibid.*, LXIX (February, 1816), p. 121.
11. *Ibid.*, LXIX (February, 1816), p. 119.
12. Sven M. Armens, *op. cit.*, p. 186.
13. *Ibid.*, p. 189.
14. See Addison's essays on true and false wit, *The Spectator*, No. 58-63, May 7-12, 1711.
15. Armens, *op. cit.*, p. 189.

Chapter Five

1. Pope to Swift, ? Jan. 1727/8, Pope, *Correspondence*, II, 469.
2. Pope, *Correspondence* II, 474.
3. See William Eben Schultz, *Gay's Beggar's Opera, Its Content, History and Influence* (New Haven, Conn., 1923), pp. 7-10.
4. *Mist's Weekly Journal*, March 30, 1728; quoted by Schultz, *op.cit.*, p. 227.
5. *Thievery A-la-mode: or The Fatal Encouragement* (London, 1728), p. 19.
6. *Ibid.*, pp. 23-24.
7. *A Satyrical Poem: Or, The Beggar's-Opera Dissected* (London, [1729]), p. 5.
8. F—— B—— L——, *The Rational Rosciad* (London, 1767), p. 12.
9. *The Gentleman's Magazine*, XLIII (1773), p. 464.
10. Sir John Hawkins, "On the Dangerous Tendency of the *Beggar's Opera*," *Universal Magazine*, LX (January, 1777), 47-48.
11. The account of this production is contained in a clipping in the collection of Ernest Lewis Gay now in the Harvard College Library. Its source is unidentified, and I have been unable to locate it.

12. *The Intelligencer,* No. 3 (London, 1729), p. 24.
13. *Ibid.,* p. 25.
14. William Henry Irving, *op. cit.,* p. 251.
15. *The Modern Poet. A Rapsody,* 2nd ed. (London, 1736), p. 13.
16. *Ibid.,* p. 14.
17. *The Plays of John Gay,* 2 vols. (London, [1923]), I, 135-36. All succeeding quotations from *The Beggar's Opera* are also from this edition.
18. *The Intelligencer,* p. 25.
19. Bertrand H. Bronson, "The Beggar's Opera," *Studies in the Literature of the Augustan Age,* ed. Richard C. Boys (Ann Arbor, Michigan, 1952), pp. 204-17.
20. *Ibid.,* p. 216.
21. *Ibid.,* p. 217.
22. Irving, *op. cit.,* p. 239.
23. William Empson, "The Beggar's Opera: Mock-Pastoral as the Cult of Independence," *Some Versions of Pastoral* (Norfolk, Conn., 1960), p. 232.
24. Bronson, *op. cit.,* p. 222.
25. Bronson, *op. cit.,* p. 223.
26. T. B. Stroup, "Gay's Mohocks and Milton," *Journal of English and Germanic Philology,* XLVI (1946), 164-67.
27. John Gay, *The Wife of Bath* (London, 1713), p. 16. This play is not included in the twentieth-century edition of Gay's plays.
28. Irving, *op. cit.,* p. 79.
29. ? Jan. 1717; Pope, *Correspondence,* I, 388.
30. Irving, *op. cit.,* p. 154.
31. *Ibid.,* p. 148.
32. John Gay, Alexander Pope, and John Arbuthnot, *Three Hours After Marriage,* ed. John Harrington Smith (Los Angeles, 1961), p. 1.
33. Samuel Johnson, "Gay," *Lives of the English Poets,* II, 69.
34. Irving, *op. cit.,* p. 303.

Chapter Six

1. "Archetype Musical," *The Guardian,* July 15, 1963, p. 7.
2. J. W. Lambert, "Beggars Behind Bars," *The Sunday Times,* July 21, 1963, p. 32.
3. Review of *The Beggar's Opera, The Spectator,* July 26, 1963, p. 110.
4. Review of *The Beggar's Opera, The Observer,* July 21, 1963, p. 23.
5. William Hazlitt, *On the English Stage,* under date July 27, 1826; quoted by William Eben Schultz, *op. cit.,* p. 274.
6. William Empson, *op. cit.,* p. 218.

7. Sven M. Armens, *op. cit.*, p. 141.
8. *Ibid.*, p. 141.
9. John Gay, *The Beggar's Opera.* A Faithful Reproduction of the 1729 Edition (Larchmont, N.Y., 1961).
10. Preface to *Polly,* quoted by Schultz, *op. cit.,* p. 211.
11. Schultz, *op. cit.,* p. 213.
12. James R. Sutherland, "'Polly' Among the Pirates," *Modern Language Review,* XXXVII (1942), 291.
13. Schultz, *op. cit.,* p. 220.
14. Sutherland, "'Polly' Among the Pirates," p. 291.
15. See *ibid.,* pp. 292-93.

Chapter Seven

1. *The Grounds of Criticism in Poetry* (London, 1704), p. 8.
2. John Gay, "*Eighteenth-Century English Literature: Modern Essays in Criticism,* ed. James L. Clifford (New York, 1959), p. 133.

Selected Bibliography

PRIMARY SOURCES

The best modern edition of Gay's works is *The Poetical Works of John Gay,* ed. G. C. Faber. London: Oxford University Press, 1926. This contains all the poems, several of the plays, and fragments of others, and is the text referred to throughout this volume; it is unfortunately out of print.

The Faber edition must be supplemented by the following works:

Gay, John. *The Beggar's Opera.* A Faithful Reproduction of the 1729 edition. Larchmont, N.Y.: Argonaut Books, 1961. Contains the original words of all the tunes Gay adapted.

The Plays of John Gay. 2 vols. Abbey Classics. London: Chapman and Dodd, [1923].

Gay, John. *The Present State of Wit (1711).* Augustan Reprint Society Publication Number 7. Los Angeles: Clark Library, 1947.

Gay, John, Alexander Pope, and John Arbuthnot. *Three Hours After Marriage,* ed. Richard Morton and William Paterson. Lake Erie College Studies, I. Painesville, Ohio, 1961.

Gay, John, Alexander Pope, and John Arbuthnot. *Three Hours After Marriage,* ed. John Harrington Smith. Augustan Reprint Society Publication Number 91-92. Los Angeles: Clark Library, 1961.

Gay, John. *The Wife of Bath.* London, 1713.

Sherburn, George, ed. *The Correspondence of Alexander Pope.* 5 vols. Oxford: Oxford University Press, 1956. Contains many of Gay's letters.

No American edition of Gay is currently in print; a definitive edition is, however, in progress, under the editorship of Vinton A. Dearing. An extensive selection from Gay is contained in *Eighteenth-Century Poetry,* ed. P. M. Spacks, Englewood Cliffs, N.Y.: Prentice-Hall, 1964.

SECONDARY SOURCES

1. Biographical

Irving, William Henry. *John Gay, Favorite of the Wits.* Durham, N.C.: Duke University Press, 1940. The best biography, thorough and informative. Critical judgments sometimes weak.

Melville, Lewis [pseud. for Lewis S. Benjamin]. *Life and Letters of John Gay*. London: D. O'Connor, 1921. Rather old-fashioned and somewhat perfunctory. Contains some interesting letters.

2. General Criticism

Armens, Sven M. *John Gay, Social Critic.* New York: King's Crown Press, 1954. The only full-length critical study of Gay, this is frequently provocative, but marred by special pleading and by failure to consider poetry something significantly different from prose.

Brown, Wallace Cable. "Gay: Pope's Alter Ego," *The Triumph of Form*. Chapel Hill: University of North Carolina Press, 1948. Considers Gay's poetic technique in his use of the couplet.

Johnson, Samuel. "Gay," *Lives of the English Poets,* ed. George Hill. 3 vols. Oxford: Clarendon Press, 1905. Biographical sketch and sharp critical commentary.

Sutherland, James. "John Gay," *Eighteenth Century English Literature: Modern Essays in Criticism,* ed. James L. Clifford. A Galaxy Book. New York: Oxford University Press, 1959. An appreciative and penetrating general analysis of Gay's poetry.

3. Criticism of *The Beggar's Opera*

Berger, A. V. "The Beggar's Opera, the Burlesque, and Italian Opera," *Music and Letters,* XVII (1936), 93-105.

Bronson, Bertrand H. "The Beggar's Opera," *Studies in the Comic,* University of California Publications in English. Vol. VIII, No. 2 (1941), 197-231. Reprinted in *Studies in the Literature of the Augustan Age,* ed. Richard C. Boys. Ann Arbor: George Wahr Publishing Co., 1952. Certainly the best critical study of the play, this essay presents a thorough general analysis and also discusses the relation of Gay's work to the tradition of Italian opera.

Empson, William. "The Beggar's Opera: Mock-Pastoral as the Cult of Independence," *Some Versions of Pastoral.* Norfolk, Conn.: New Directions, 1960. A provocative, highly individual discussion.

Schultz, William Eben. *Gay's Beggar's Opera, Its Content, History and Influence*. New Haven: Yale University Press, 1923. An exhaustive but essentially uncritical study, valuable for defining sources and influences of Gay's play.

Sherwin, J. J. "The World Is Mean and Man Uncouth," *Vir-*

ginia Quarterly Review, XXXV (1959), 258-70. A comparative analysis of certain ideas in *The Beggar's Opera* and in *The Threepenny Opera.*

4. Criticism of Other Individual Works

Aden, John M. "The 1720 Version of *Rural Sports* and the Georgic Tradition," *Modern Language Quarterly,* XX (1959), 228-32. Discusses changes between first and second version of poem in light of Gay's attitude toward Virgilian tradition.

Ellis, William D., Jr., "Thomas D'Urfey, the Pope-Philips Quarrel, and *The Shepherd's Week,*" *Publications of the Modern Language Association,* LXXIV (1959), 203-12. Discussion of the elements of parody in Gay's pastorals.

Moore, John Robert. "Gay's Burlesque of Sir Richard Blackmore's Poetry," *Journal of English and Germanic Philology,* L (1951), 83-89. Suggests another object of parody, particularly in *The Shepherd's Week.*

Stroup, T. B. "Gay's Mohocks and Milton," *Journal of English and Germanic Philology,* XLVI (1946), 164-67. Points out Gay's use of Miltonic reference and style in *The Mohocks.*

Swaen, A. E. H. "The Airs and Tunes of John Gay's *Polly,*" *Anglia,* LX (1936), 403-22. Identifies fully the tunes which Gay adapted.

Trowbridge, Hoyt. "Pope, Gay, and *The Shepherd's Week,*" *Modern Language Quarterly,* V (1944), 79-88. A balanced analysis of Gay's place in the Pope-Philips quarrel over pastoral.

Wells, Henry W. "The Seven Against London" *Sewanee Review,* XLVII (1939), 514-23. A long poem in heroic couplets which attempts to define the satiric attitudes of seven eighteenth-century poets. Gay's *Fables* are treated.

Sutherland, James R. " 'Polly' Among the Pirates," *Modern Language Review,* XXXVII (1942), 291-303. A discussion of the history of early piracies of *Polly.*

Index